Songs
of Zion

13 42 C. B

13 46 C B

Songs of Zion

Supplemental Worship Resources 12

Abingdon Press
Nashville
1981

Songs of Zion

Copyright © 1981, 1982 Abingdon

Fifth printing 1983

Library of Congress Cataloging in Publication Data

Main entry under title:
Songs of Zion.
  (Supplemental worship resources: 12)
  Hymns, with music.
  1. Hymns, English. 2. United Methodist Church
  (United States)—Hymns.
  M2127.S65   783.9'52   81-8039   AACR2

ISBN 0-687-39120-2

ISBN 0-687-39121-0 (Accompanist's Edition)

Book Designer: Leonardo M. Ferguson

Copy Editor: Mada P. Johnston

Music set by the Staff of Better Music Type, Nashville, Tenn.
Laurens A. Blankers, Owner

MANUFACTURED BY THE PARTHENON PRESS AT
NASHVILLE, TENNESSEE, UNITED STATES OF AMERICA

Contents

Acknowledgments

Acknowledgment is made to all individuals and establishments who have granted permission for the use of copyrighted material for this volume.

A very special acknowledgment is made to Mrs. Gertrude Ward and to Mrs. Willa Ward Royster, respectively mother and sister of the late Clara Ward, who granted exclusive permission for the use of compositions contained herein by Clara Ward, which are no longer in print.

Acknowledgment is made to the following persons on the Board of Discipleship who expended time beyond their normal duties to see that this project was successfully completed: Mrs. Elise Shoemaker, Ms. Lois Pottle, Mrs. Dorothy Turner-Lacy, and Dr. Hoyt L. Hickman.

A very special thanks to Dr. William B. McClain, Chairman of the National Advisory Task Force for the project, for his sound advice, literary contributions, and unmitigated dedication to the life of the project.

A very special thanks to the Reverend Fletcher J. Bryant, former Assistant General Secretary of the Board of Discipleship who initially recommended that this project be undertaken, for his continued dedication and support after its inception.

Sincere gratitude is graciously extended to Mrs. Angela S. Powell and to Mrs. Juanita E. Holiday who served as secretaries for the Editors throughout the life of the project.

Acknowledgment is made to the following persons at The United Methodist Publishing House who believed in the project and whose dedicated efforts substantiated those beliefs: Robert O. Hoffelt, Charles O. McNish, Ronald P. Patterson, John Procter, and Gwendolyn Pullen.

Credits

The historical accounts of the Hymn and Black Gospel were written by Dr. J. Jefferson Cleveland.

The historical account of the Negro Spiritual was written by Dr. J. Jefferson Cleveland, in collaboration with Dr. William B. McClain.

The National Advisory
Task Force on the Hymnbook Project

William B. McClain, Chairman
J. Jefferson Cleveland, Editor
Verolga Nix, Editor

Fletcher J. Bryant
Cynthia Felder
Douglass E. Fitch
Donald Gilmore
Howard M. Ham
Hoyt L. Hickman
Zan Holmes, Jr.

Charlotte A. Meade
Maceo Pembroke
Israel Rucker
Forrest Stith
Ethel Lou Talbert
Melvin G. Talbert

*   *   *   *

The Section on Worship of the Board of Discipleship has given editorial oversight to the project and has approved *Songs of Zion* as the 12th publication in its Supplemental Worship Resources (SWR Series). The Section consists of Louise H. Schown (chairperson), James F. White (chairperson, editorial committee), Bishop Robert E. Goodrich, Paul F. Abel, Phyllis Close, Edward L. Duncan, Judy Gilreath, Kay Hereford, Judith Kelsey-Powell, Marilyn Maybee, L. Doyle Masters, William B. McClain, Carlton R. Young, and Janet Lee (ex officio).

Section on Worship staff included Melvin G. Talbert, Roberto Escamilla, Hoyt L. Hickman, Richard L. Eslinger, and Elsie M. Shoemaker.

Preface

Growing out of the Consultation on the Black Church in Atlanta, Georgia, in 1973, sponsored by the Board of Discipleship, was a specific recommendation that the Section on Worship develop a songbook from the Black religious tradition to be made available to United Methodist churches. This urgent recommendation was made by a workshop on worship I conducted after we carefully surveyed the present *Book of Hymns* only to find it contains only one hymn by a Black composer and a mere five Negro spirituals, listed simply as "American Folk Hymns." This songbook, entitled *Songs of Zion,* is the realization of the dream of those persons who gathered in Atlanta eight years ago.

The Black religious tradition in America, while unique to Black Americans, can contribute much and has made a vast difference in the Christian church in this nation. For it has been Black people's understanding of God in the context of their own experience, i.e., the Black experience, in which they have groped for meaning, relevance, worth, assurance, reconciliation, and their proper response to the God revealed in nature and in Jesus Christ. And whatever point of the history of Black people and their religion in America one may wish to view, the gathering of the community in worship and praise to Almighty God is central and pivotal to what happens afterward. It is the fulcrum of the souls of Black folks.

A very real part of the worship of Black people is the songs of Zion. Singing is as close to worship as breathing is to life. These songs of the soul and of the soil have helped to bring a people through the torture chambers of the last three centuries. They reflect the truth of an old African dictum: "The Spirit will not descend without song."

The Spirit has descended often when slaves and ex-slaves have gathered in worship and sung the Negro spirituals. These spirituals reveal the rich culture and the ineffable beauty and creativity of the Black soul and intimate the uniqueness of the Black religious tradition. These spirituals speak of life and death, suffering and sorrow, love and judgment, grace and hope, justice and mercy. They are the songs of an unhappy people, a people weary at heart, a discontent people, and yet they are the most beautiful expression of human experience and faith this side of the seas.

The music probably predates the words. The words are the siftings of centuries. They tell of exile and trouble, of strife and hiding; they grope for liberation and rest and aid from some unseen power. But as W. E. B. DuBois points out: "Through all the sorrow songs there breathes a hope, a faith in the ultimate justice of things." They oppose racism and long for a racially just society where human equality under the sovereignty of God is achieved. They are not simply songs, but principles and a point of view. And these principles and point of view become the bedrock of a religious tradition: God is on the side of the oppressed.

The gospel song was created in the North. It became the Northern counterpart of the Negro spiritual of the South. It is a combination of the sheer joy of living and deep religious faith. It arose amid the early exodus from the farmlands and hamlets of the South, when Black people arrived in Chicago and New York and Detroit and other Northern cities and found themselves in a strange land. Again, the songs of Zion were on their lips. The simple lines of the gospel were written on their minds and hearts and got translated into praise in their mouths. It was the faith that inspired the song and not the song that created the faith.

The gospel song expresses theology. Not the theology of the academy or the university, not formalistic theology or the theology of the seminary, but a *theology of experience*—the theology of a God who sends the sunshine and the rain, the theology of a God who is very much alive and active and who has not forsaken those who are poor and oppressed and unemployed. It is a *theology of imagination*—it grew out of fire shut up in the bones, of words painted on the canvas of the mind. Fear is turned to hope in the sanctuaries and storefronts, and bursts forth in songs of celebration. It is a *theology of grace* that allows the faithful to see the sunshine of His face—even through their tears. Even the words of an ex-slave trader become a song of liberation and an expression of God's amazing grace. It is a *theology of survival* that allows a people to celebrate the ability to continue the journey in spite of the insidious tentacles of racism and oppression and to sing, "It's another day's journey, and I'm glad about it!"

These songs of the Black religious tradition have enriched Western Christianity. They have provided spiritual strength and moral stamina for facing present realities without succumbing, while presenting the eternal perspective that gives meaning to the struggle.

The songs of Zion are the voices of the soul. They reflect the past of slavery and servitude, the struggle for freedom and liberation; they reflect the present with its continuing demands and perplexities and an ever-present hope for a future that will reflect the rulership of God over the principalities and powers.

But the Black experience in America is a multifaceted experience encompassing numerous aspects of an Americn experience and a way of life. No accurate picture of the history of America can be presented without attention to the experience of Black people. No complete picture of Black people can be given without due attention to the Black religious tradition. This book presents that past in songs. The introductions to each section help us understand those songs. Not only did Black people compose gospel songs and spirituals, but often the hymns of the faith and other religious songs got transposed and arranged and sung as new songs of Zion. They are included here, for they were a part of the Black religious tradition in the same way that the Greek tragedies were a part of creative genius of the plays of Shakespeare.

And songs of Zion continue. Many new hymns and liberation songs and gospel songs have been composed by contemporary artists who are aware of that tradition and who are steeped in its heritage. Chants and introits, anthems and responses composed or arranged by these church musicians are a valuable addition and enrichment to the songs of Zion.

This songbook offers the whole church a volume of songs that can enrich the worship of the whole church. It is music that has nourished a people, soothed their hurts, sustained their hopes, and bound their wounds. It is music that will broaden the musical genres in worship in any Christian church. It is the songs of Zion to be sung by God's people, who are always strangers and pilgrims in any land they inhabit. Every land they inhabit is theirs, and every land is foreign. For we are pilgrims, but we can sing the songs of Zion in a strange land.

These songs are offered on the altar of the church by a people, who, while in this strange land, sang the songs of Zion to the glory of God.

William B. McClain
Associate Professor
Homiletics and Worship

Wesley Theological Seminary
Washington, D.C.

Keys to Musical Interpretation, Performance, and Meaningful Worship

General Suggestions

DIRECTOR

Proper musical performance and interpretation are aids to meaningful worship experiences.

Music is an important part of the worship service, so be sensitive to the worship leader.

Worship is a total experience, and many worship through the musical word as well as through the spoken word.

Sometimes the place of a song in the worship service can say much about the tempo. For example, the refrain to the hymn, "I Surrender All," may be used as a prayer chant, in which case it would be performed slower than usual.

Be creative and add other instruments, such as guitars, drums, and tambourines, to performances, but use discretion in doing so. Don't overdo it! Hand clapping can also be very effective with certain music genres.

ACCOMPANIST (PIANIST or ORGANIST)

Accompanying is an important role, so pay close attention to the director, soloist, and worship leader.

If no one is directing the congregation, it is left to the accompanist to *lead* with his or her instrument, so lead forcefully.

Be careful of playing too loudly. It can overpower the singing or detract from a worshipful mood.

The use of modulation between verses (thereby singing the next verse of the hymn or composition in a new key) adds variety and stimulates the congregation.

CONGREGATION

Sing with exuberance! New songs should be sung with as much vigor and vitality as old songs.

When the mouth is open wide, the vocal mechanisms function more freely and easier. Vowel sounds should be long and intense, while consonant sounds should be short and distinct.

Blend your voices. Do not strive to be heard above everyone else by singing too loudly.

Sing *with* the director, choirs, and instruments but not before or after them.

The instrumental introduction of a song is preparation for setting the following:
-pitch (starting tones)
-tempo (fast, slow, or moderate)
-mood (prayerfuly, lively, etc.)

All songs should not be sung the same way. Close attention should be given to the mood as indicated by the words and tempo. For example, "God Is So Good" should be sung quite differently from "Lift Him Up."

The words of a composition can sometimes dictate the tempo.

There is a message in the text (words) of each song, so concentrate and sing accordingly.

Close attention should be paid to the rhythm of the song, for, in many instances, sixteenth (♫) or thirty-second (♬) notes are only to indicate slurs or inflections of the voice.

Specific Suggestions
Pertaining to *Songs of Zion*

INSTRUMENTAL IMPROVISATION

The *beat* (rhythm) is one of the most important aspects of Black music, whether the composition is fast, slow, or moderate. It must be kept as soon as it is established. Sometimes the beat (rhythm) will change while the performance is in progress and then revert to the original beat. No matter what, keep whatever beat is established at any given time.

There are very few moments of silence in instrumental improvisation of Black music, and when they do occur they are generally for special effects. Fill in all measures of rests (or open spaces) with chords duplicated at the upper or lower octave, broken chords (arpeggios), passing tones either as single notes or in octaves, passing tone chords, upper and lower neighboring tones, runs, turns, glissandi, chromatic motives or phrases, and so on. Remember, however, that all these "extras" must be utilized with taste and discretion. Whatever the nature of your improvisation, *do not* leave open spaces.

The changing of keys (modulation) is very common in Black music performance. It adds variety and often heightens the emotional effect of the composition. In most instances, a half or whole step change of key or a series (succession) of half or whole step changes will suffice. However, there are no restrictions in this area of improvisation.

Most compositions can be reduced to a I-IV-V-I chord progression, whether they are written in a major or minor key. Therefore, chordal embellishment or decoration is very common in Black music performance. Use augmented tonic and dominant chords; dominant chords; secondary dominant chords; diminished triads; dominant, augmented, and diminished seventh chords; ninth, eleventh, and thirteenth chords; chordal inversions; and altered chords.

Flatted thirds, sixths, and sevenths are common. Use them.

The common cadences appear in Black music, but deceptive ones are also frequently used. V-VI, V-IV, and I-V^7/II-V^7-I are common. Delayed chordal resolutions and chord-pedals are also very common.

Spontaneity (improvisation) does not necessarily mean lack of rehearsal.

VOCAL IMPROVISATION

Vocal improvisation consists mainly of embellishment of the melodic line and is usually left up to the vocalist(s). This process usually consists of slurs, runs, shouts, extra-long held notes, turns, chromaticisms, flatted thirds, sixths, sevenths, and so forth. When vocal improvisation is being engaged in, instrumental improvisation should be subdued.

TEXTS

Alternative texts found in *Songs of Zion* are incorporated within the composition or are presented at the bottom of the composition for:
—clarity of meaning or thought
—deletion of sexist language

VOCAL GENRES IN *SONGS OF ZION*

Hymns

Most of the hymns can be improvised, if desired.

These hymns may often be used as special selections by arranging and/or rearranging, so do not hesitate to use *Songs of Zion* and other available resources.

In metering or "lining out" a hymn such as "Father, I Stretch My Hands to Thee," the first phrase is spoken or chanted by one person before everyone responds.

Example:

Leader: *(spoken or chanted)* "Father, I stretch my hands to Thee; no other help I know; . . ."
Response: *(chanted or sung)* "Father, I stretch . . ." etc.

In the lined-out hymns, simultaneous embellishment of the basic melody is highly recommended.

These hymns (like all hymns) should be:
—rehearsed during regular rehearsal periods,
—taught during the morning service or at special services such as hymn-fests,
—rehearsed as anthems are, by taking them apart and teaching the parts.

Negro Spirituals

Perform these compositions as written; however, many can be improvised to a restricted degree without distorting their overall effect.

Pay close attention to the *dialect*. Do not change it into correct English or overexaggerate it because both would *destroy* the intent of the composition, as well as its performance.

a. General guidelines to follow when using dialect:
(1) The dialect should be articulated as clearly as you would sing the words in other songs.
(2) The English words "the," "this," and "that" in dialect would become "de," "dis," and "dat." "De" is usually pronounced "dee" before vowels and "duh" before consonants:

Examples:
"De" *("Dee")* Ol' Ark's A-Moverin'
I Been In "De" *("Duh")* Storm

(3) Sometimes the words of the song are altered to fit the rhythm of the music. Thus "children" may become "chillun" or "chil-dun"; "heaven" may become "heb'm," "heb'n," or "hev'n"; "Lord" may become "Lawd," "Lo'd," or "Lohd."
(4) Handclapping may be used.

Black Gospels

Use unrestricted improvisation, for the written manuscripts basically are guides to the format of the songs. Very few gospel songs are written down the way they should sound. Improvisation, both vocal and instrumental, is highly recommended.

Handclapping is highly recommended.

Songs for Special Occasions

Do not improvise these songs. Perform them as written.

Service Music

Compositions written in the Black idiom may be improvised, if desired. *Do not* improvise those compositions written in the European, "classical" style—perform these as written.

A Historical Account of the Hymn in the Black Worship Experience

The definition of the hymn has presented difficulties since the earliest times. For St. Augustine it was "the praise of God by singing." If one of the three elements implied in this definition—namely, praise, devotion to God, or song—is lacking, then there is, according to Augustine, no hymn. But this definition also covers psalms and canticles and we can further define the hymn if we add a fourth necessary element—that it should be sung by the congregation.[1]

The hymn as we know it and sing it today could be technically defined as a song of adoration and praise to God. "In the early Christian era, the term 'hymn' was applied to all songs in praise of the Lord."[2]

In the United States, prior to 1730, psalms and canticles, which were more a part of Gregorian chants, were the most prevalent type of congregational singing used in the colonial church. It should be noted, however, that during the colonial period (1607–1790) Blacks, slave and free, often worshiped in churches with the Whites, and sang the same music.

During the 1730's the "Great Awakening" movement brought with it a demand for the use of livelier music [than psalms and canticles] in the worship service. These new "livelier" songs were called *hymns*. This new style of texts by Dr. Isaac Watts (1674–1748) and Charles Wesley (1707–1788) appealed to Blacks because of the vitality of the words, wider use of intervals than in the psalm tunes, and their rhythmic freedom. The book *Hymns and Spiritual Songs* published by Dr. Watts in 1707 and a *Collection of Psalms and Hymns* (1742) published by the Reverend John Wesley (1703–1791) together with his brother the Rev. Charles Wesley, became most widely used, and the latter book ultimately became the forerunner of the official Methodist Hymnal.[3]

These tune books, sometimes in three- and four-part harmony, were basically intended for unison singing by the congregation. It is most interesting to note that the tune books either had no text at all or simply used the first stanza of the hymn, while the singers used a separate hymnal which contained the remaining stanzas. Although these hymnals were put together by ministers of a particular denomination, they were in fact designed to be used by Christians of all denominations.

---

1. The *Larousse Encyclopedia of Music,* ed. Geoffrey Hindley (Secaucus, N.J.: Chartwell Books, 1976), p. 60.
2. Willi Apel, *Harvard Dictionary of Music* (Cambridge: Harvard University Press, 1977), p. 397.
3. Eileen Southern, *The Music of Black Americans* (New York: W. W. Norton, 1971), p. 40.

Toward the end of the eighteenth century, Blacks began to break away from the White congregations and establish their own places of worship. They brought to their own worship service semblances of the White church in format; however, the music gained another dimension by the addition of their own indigenous experiences. The creation of new musical forms began—the Black hymn and spiritual.

Music, especially singing, has always been an integral part of the Black church worship service, just as the Black church has always been a "church of emotion." It was the African culture that bequeathed these religious practices to Afro-Christian worship and to Afro-American culture. When Blacks began to establish their own churches, they did not discard the sophisticated hymns learned from their experiences in White Christian worship; rather, many of these hymns were adopted and converted into original Black songs. These "made-over" White hymns were the results of diverse influences including: (1) African religious music, (2) the African call-and-response song, (3) European or American religious and secular songs, and (4) various African and Afro-American dialects. And how were they made over? The melodies were often improvised to fit the needs of the Black worship service. On the other hand, many of these melodies were kept intact, but the rhythms and harmonies of these hymns and songs were changed to reflect the Black worship experience; consequently, many hymns from the Watts, Wesley, Sankey, and other hymnals were molded into a strictly Black idiom. Cases in point are: John Newton's "Amazing Grace," Fanny Crosby's "Jesus, Keep Me Near the Cross," Charles Wesley's "Jesus, Lover of My Soul,"[4] Thomas Moore's "Come, Ye Disconsolate," William Bradbury's "Just As I Am," Fannie Crosby's "Close to Thee," D. A. J. Showalter's "Leaning on the Everlasting Arms," and Isaac Watts' "The Day Is Past and Gone."

Not until the beginning of the twentieth century do we see the emergence of Blacks who became prolific as hymn writers in the Afro-American style. These compositions were gospel songs in the conventional sense—not gospel songs in the contemporary style, but tabernacle and revival songs. They lacked the emotional zeal that is so characteristic of the contemporary gospel and are appropriately called *gospel hymns.*

Without a doubt, the renowned Dr. Charles Albert Tindley (1856–1933) was the most prolific of the Black hymn writers. He was for more than thirty years the outstanding pastor of the famous Tindley Temple United Methodist Church in Philadelphia, Pennsylvania.

In 1924, the membership of East Calvary Methodist Episcopal Church insisted that the church's name be changed to Tindley Temple in honor of its illustrious pastor and hymn writer. Dr. Tindley's productive period as a composer was 1901–1906, but his music did not become generally popular in Black churches until after World War I. Nevertheless, it was Dr. Tindley's music that inspired the famous gospel

---

4. Clint Bonner, *A Hymn Is Born* (Nashville: Broadman Press, 1959), "Jesus, Lover of My Soul," pp. 19-21.

songwriter Dr. Thomas A. Dorsey (1899–) to forsake the vaudeville and blues circuits and write religious music exclusively.

Tindley's gospel hymns comprised an entirely new genre, and he readily admitted that they leaned heavily on the Negro spiritual. Tindley incorporated folk images, proverbs, and biblical allusions well-known to Black Christians for over a hundred years; yet his songs had profound universal appeal to the human heart, with words of hope, cheer, love, and pity.[5]

Several examples may be cited:

> Courage, my soul, and let us journey on,
> Tho' the night is dark it won't be very long . . .
>
> *Refrain:*
>
> Hallelujah! Hallelujah! The storm is passing over,
> Hallelujah!
> (from "The Storm Is Passing Over")

The poor and downtrodden have often found solace in a specific address to them from Tindley:

> *Refrain:*
> Leave it there, leave it there,
> Take your burden to the Lord and leave it there,
> If you trust and never doubt,
> He will surely bring you out,
> Take your burden to the Lord and leave it there.
> (from "Leave It There")

Ultimate happiness and peace will be ours someday if we just "keep the faith," says Tindley:

> Beams of heaven, as I go,
> Thro' this wilderness below,
> Guide my feet in peaceful ways,
> Turn my midnights into days.
> When in the darkness I would grope,
> Faith always sees a star of hope,
> And soon from all life's grief and danger,
> I shall be free some day.
>
> *Refrain:*
> I do not know how long 'twill be,
> Nor what the future holds for me,
> But this I know, if Jesus leads me,
> I shall get home some day.
> (from "Beams of Heaven")

---

5. Tony Heilbut, *The Gospel Sound* (New York: Simon & Schuster, 1971), p. 58.

The refrain to another Tindley hymn was easily transformed into the greatest of all freedom songs:

> *Original version:*
> I'll overcome some day, I'll overcome some day;
> If in my heart I do not yield, I'll overcome some day.
>   (from "I'll Overcome Some Day")
>
> *Transformed version:*
> We shall overcome, we shall overcome
> We shall overcome some day;
> Oh, if in our hearts, we do not yield,
> We shall overcome some day.
>   (from freedom song "We Shall Overcome")

Tindley's greatest hymn combines the emotion of an Isaac Watts hymn with that of a Black spiritual. It, too, is an explicit example of the use of blue modes, jazz syncopations, and avenues of improvisation:

> When the storms of life are raging, stand by me,
> When the storms of life are raging, stand by me,
> When the world is tossing me,
> Like a ship upon the sea,
> Thou who rulest wind and water, stand by me.
>   (from "Stand by Me")

The Rev. Dr. Charles Albert Tindley was an outstanding and world-renowned minister, and Tindley Temple United Methodist Church[6] stands today as a tangible memorial to his ministry. He ministered not only through the spoken word; he ministered through song and was an astute and prolific composer, and his numerous hymns remain as self-memorials to his ministry through music. He, by his love of God and his devotion to humanity, won the hearts not only of the City of Brotherly Love, but the hearts of many throughout the United States and the world. Not bad for a one-time slave and hod-carrier! He bequeathed to all Methodism and to Christianity a legacy that will live on through his hymns.

Despite the fact that Tindley's gospel hymns grew mainly out of the Black experience, they possess strong universal appeal. They can be performed as hymns but can be easily converted into contemporary gospel songs that remain useful to all races.

Evidence of the influence of Tindley's hymn style can be seen in the works of contemporary hymn writers such as James Hendrix, Richard Alan Henderson, and Morris C. Queen, representing a group of young composers who recognize the need to preserve the Tindley style and who incorporate this style into their own varied compositional techniques.

                                                              J. Jefferson Cleveland

---

6. Tindley Temple United Methodist Church, Broad and Fitzwater Streets, Philadelphia, Pennsylvania 19146.

Glory Be to Our God on High

DUKE STREET
John Hatton, d.1793

William M. James, 1915-

Majestically

1. Glo - ry be to our God on high, Sang hosts of an - gels long a - go. These great her - alds brought Je - sus nigh, To the place we long to go.
2. Come, Lord and Sav - ior, to us now. In ev - 'ry heart Thy room pre - pare. Bless us that we be - fore Thee bow, As shep-herds by the man - ger there.
3. Has - ten the day Thy King - dom, Lord, Shall be com-plet - ed ev - 'ry - where. Spread-ing the news of Je - sus' birth Prais - ing Thee for Thy lov - ing care. A - men.

3 We're Marching to Zion

Isaac Watts, 1674-1748
Refrain by R.L.

MARCHING TO ZION
Robert Lowry, 1826-1899

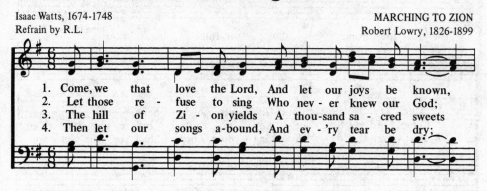

1. Come, we that love the Lord, And let our joys be known,
2. Let those re - fuse to sing Who nev - er knew our God;
3. The hill of Zi - on yields A thou-sand sa - cred sweets
4. Then let our songs a-bound, And ev - 'ry tear be dry;

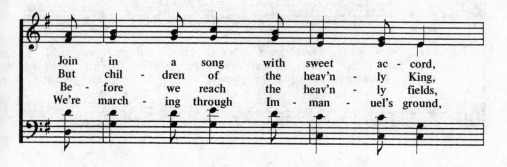

Join in a song with sweet ac - cord,
But chil - dren of the heav'n - ly King,
Be - fore we reach the heav'n - ly fields,
We're march - ing through Im - man - uel's ground,

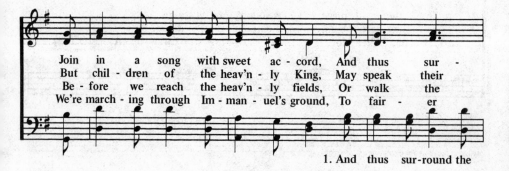

Join in a song with sweet ac - cord, And thus sur -
But chil - dren of the heav'n - ly King, May speak their
Be - fore we reach the heav'n - ly fields, Or walk the
We're march - ing through Im - man - uel's ground, To fair - er

1. And thus sur-round the

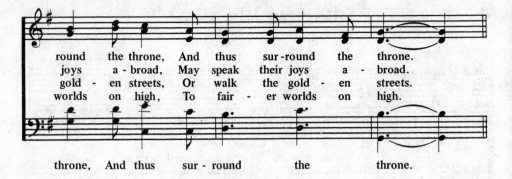

round   the throne,   And   thus   sur-round   the   throne.
joys   a - broad,   May   speak   their joys   a -   broad.
gold - en streets,   Or   walk   the gold - en   streets.
worlds   on high,   To   fair - er worlds   on   high.

throne,   And thus   sur - round   the   throne.

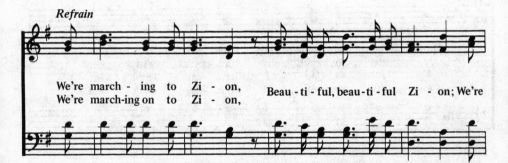

Refrain

We're march - ing   to   Zi - on,   Beau - ti - ful, beau - ti - ful   Zi - on; We're
We're march-ing on   to   Zi - on,

march-ing up-ward to   Zi - on,   The beau-ti-ful cit-y   of God.
                 Zi - on, Zi - on,

4 Glory to His Name

Elisha A. Hoffman, 1839-1929

GLORY TO HIS NAME
John H. Stockton, 1813-1877

1. Down at the cross where my Sav - ior died,
2. I am so won - drous - ly saved from sin,
3. O pre - cious foun - tain that saves from sin,
4. Come to this foun - tain so rich and sweet,

Down where for cleans - ing from sin I cried,
Je - sus so sweet - ly a - bides with - in;
I am so glad I have en - tered in;
Cast thy poor soul at the Sav - ior's feet;

There to my heart was the blood ap - plied;
There at the cross where He took me in;
There Je - sus saves me and keeps me clean;
Plunge in to - day, and be made com - plete;
} Glo - ry to His name.

Refrain

Glo - ry to His name, Glo - ry to His name;

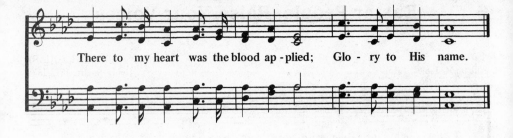

There to my heart was the blood ap-plied; Glo-ry to His name.

All Is Well

5

J.H.

James Hendrix, 1920-

Slow, with expression

1. Look-ing back through the years, there were joys and some tears.
2. Days of la - bor were long; grace from God kept us strong.

There were loss - es and gains; there was laugh-ter and some pains.
At the close of life's day, Shep-herd hands will lead the way.

Refrain

All is well, all is well, all is well, all is well.

6   Easter People, Raise Your Voices

William M. James, 1915-

REGENT SQUARE
Henry Smart, 1813-1879

Joyously

1. Eas - ter peo - ple, raise your voic - es, Sounds of heav'n in
2. Fear of death can no more stop us, From our press - ing
3. Ev - 'ry day to us is Eas - ter, With its Res - ur -

earth should ring. Christ has brought us heav - en's choic - es
here be - low. For our Lord has now em - pow'red us
rec - tion song. When in trou - ble move the fast - er

Heav'n - ly mu - sic, let it ring. Al - le - lu - ia!
To tri - umph o - ver ev - 'ry foe. Al - le - lu - ia!
To our God who rights the wrong. Al - le - lu - ia!

Al - le - lu - ia! Eas - ter peo - ple, let us sing.
Al - le - lu - ia! On to vic - t'ry now we go.
Al - le - lu - ia! See the pow'r of heav'n - ly throngs. A - men.

Close to Thee

Fanny J. Crosby, 1820-1915

Silas J. Vail, 1818-1884

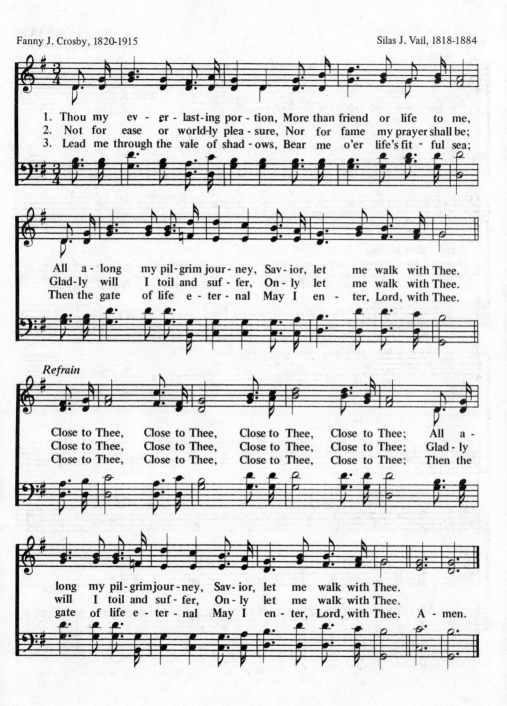

1. Thou my ev - er - last-ing por - tion, More than friend or life to me,
2. Not for ease or world-ly plea - sure, Nor for fame my prayer shall be;
3. Lead me through the vale of shad - ows, Bear me o'er life's fit - ful sea;

All a - long my pil-grim jour - ney, Sav - ior, let me walk with Thee.
Glad-ly will I toil and suf - fer, On - ly let me walk with Thee.
Then the gate of life e - ter - nal May I en - ter, Lord, with Thee.

Refrain

Close to Thee, Close to Thee, Close to Thee, Close to Thee; All a -
Close to Thee, Close to Thee, Close to Thee, Close to Thee; Glad - ly
Close to Thee, Close to Thee, Close to Thee, Close to Thee; Then the

long my pil - grim jour - ney, Sav - ior, let me walk with Thee.
will I toil and suf - fer, On - ly let me walk with Thee.
gate of life e - ter - nal May I en - ter, Lord, with Thee. A - men.

8 At the Cross

Issac Watts, 1674-1748
Refrain, R.E.H.

HUDSON
Ralph E. Hudson, 1843-1901

A - las! and did my Sav - ior bleed, And did my Sov-ereign die?
Was it for crimes that I have done, He groaned up - on the tree?
Well might the sun in dark-ness hide, And shut its glo - ries in,
But drops of grief can ne'er re - pay The debt of love I owe;

Would He de - vote that sa - cred head For sin - ners such as I?
A - maz - ing pit - y! Grace un-known! And love be - yond de - gree!
When Christ, the Might - y Mak - er, died For hu - man crea-tures' sin.
Here, Lord, I give my - self a - way 'Tis all that I can do!

Refrain

At the cross, at the cross where I first saw the light, And the
bur - den of my heart rolled a - way, rolled a-way, It was there by faith

I re-ceived my sight, And now I am hap-py all the day!

Prayer for Families

9

DAISY

Lois Stanley

Morris C. Queen, 1921 -

1. Dear Sav - ior, let thy gra-cious peace Our homes and fam-ilies
2. May all that's joy - ful, all that's pain Be shared and brought to
3. To - geth - er work, to - geth - er grow, All child - like in our

bless; Let love a - kin to thine in - crease, That bonds of ten - der-
thee. In thy deep cru - ci - ble we gain New life, new sight, and
need. May all the years thou dost be - stow, Con - firm and strength - en

ness ne'er cease Through - out life's wea - ry stress.
leave the bane, From sin and sor - row free. A - men.
all we know Of peace and joy in thee.

10 Some Day

Charles A. Tindley, 1851-1933
Arr. by F.A. Clark

C.A.T.

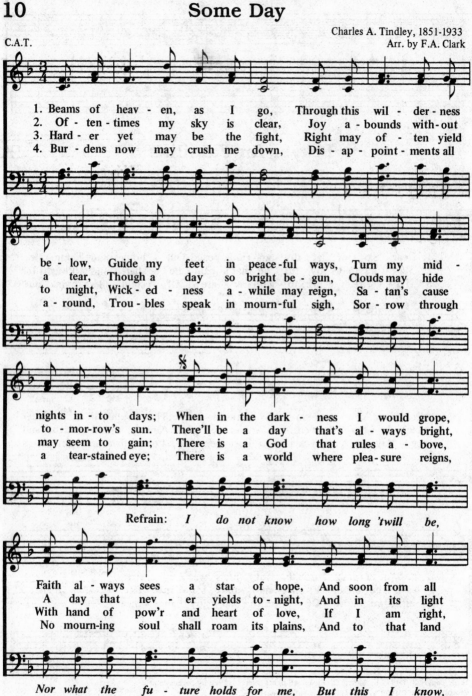

1. Beams of heav - en, as I go, Through this wil - der - ness
2. Of - ten - times my sky is clear, Joy a - bounds with - out
3. Hard - er yet may be the fight, Right may of - ten yield
4. Bur - dens now may crush me down, Dis - ap - point - ments all

be - low, Guide my feet in peace - ful ways, Turn my mid -
a tear, Though a day so bright be - gun, Clouds may hide
to might, Wick - ed - ness a - while may reign, Sa - tan's cause
a - round, Trou - bles speak in mourn - ful sigh, Sor - row through

nights in - to days; When in the dark - ness I would grope,
to - mor-row's sun. There'll be a day that's al - ways bright,
may seem to gain; There is a God that rules a - bove,
a tear-stained eye; There is a world where plea - sure reigns,

Refrain: *I do not know how long 'twill be,*

Faith al - ways sees a star of hope, And soon from all
A day that nev - er yields to - night, And in its light
With hand of pow'r and heart of love, If I am right,
No mourn-ing soul shall roam its plains, And to that land

Nor what the fu - ture holds for me, But this I know,

life's grief and dan - ger, I shall be free some day.
the streets of glo - ry I shall be - hold some day.
He'll fight my bat - tle, I shall have peace some day.
of peace and glo - ry I want to go some day.

if Je - sus leads me, I shall get home some day.

Father, I Stretch My Hands to Thee — 11

MARTYRDOM
Hugh Wilson, 1766-1824
Lined by J. Jefferson Cleveland, 1937-
and Verolga Nix, 1933-

Charles Wesley, 1707-1788

Very slowly

1. Fa - ther, I stretch my hands to Thee, No oth -
2. What did Thine on - ly Son en - dure, Be - fore
3. Sure - ly Thou canst not let me die, O speak
4. Au - thor of faith! to Thee I lift My wear -

er help I know; If Thou with - draw Thy - self
I drew my breath! What pain, what la - bor to
and I shall live; And here I will un - wear -
y, long - ing eyes; O let me now re - ceive

from me, Ah! whith - er shall I go?
se - cure My soul from end - less death!
ied lie, Till Thou Thy spir - it give.
that gift! My soul with - out it dies.

Arr. copyright © 1979 by J. Jefferson Cleveland and Verolga Nix.

12 Prayer for Africa

English by Katherine F. Rohrbough
Swahili from Ngethe Njroje
Original Zulu by Enoch Sontonga

Enoch Sontonga
Arr. by Walter F. Anderson

With dignity

English Bless, O Lord, our coun-try, Af - ri - ca, So that she may wak - en
Swahili Bwa-na, i - ba - ri - ki Af - ri - ka, I - li - i - pa - te
Zulu Nko - si, si - kel - el' i Af - ri - ka, Mal - u - pa-kam' u - pon -

from her sleep. Fill her horn with plen - ty, guide her feet.
ku - am - ka. Ma - om - bi ye tu ya - si - ki lel.
do - lway - o; Yi - va im - i - tan - da - zo ye - tu.

Hear us, faith-ful sons.* Spir - it, de-scend, (Spir-it, Spir-it,)
U - tu - ba - ri - ki. U - je Ro-ho, (U - je, U - je,)
U - si - si-kel-el - e, Yih - la Moy-a, (Yih - la Moy - a,)

* "ones" may be substituted for sons.

From *Sing It Again.* Copyright © 1958, World Around Songs. Used by permission.

Spir - it, de-scend, Spir - it, de-scend, Spir -it di - vine.
U - je Ro-ho, U - je Ro -ho, U - tu-ja - ze.
Yih - la Moy - a, Oy - ing cwel - e.

THE ORIGIN OF "NKOSI SIELEL'I AFRIKA"

Nkos Sikele' i Afrika was composed in 1897 and first publicly sung in 1899. The composition has a somewhat melancholy strain. The black folk around Johannesburg were, at the time, far from happy. The piece was commonly sung in native day schools and further popularized by the Ohlange Zulu Choir that visited the Rand giving concerts.

When the African National Congress flourished, its leaders adopted this piece as a closing anthem for their meetings, and this soon became a custom in the other provinces in connection with all types of Bantu organizations. Of late the black races of the Union and the Protectorates have somehow by tacit assent adopted it as their recognized national anthem, sung before royalty and on big public occasions.

The Day Is Past and Gone 13

Traditional

J. Jefferson Cleveland, 1937-

1. The day is past and gone, The eve-ning shades ap - pear;
2. We lay our gar - ments by Up - on our beds to rest;
3. Lord, keep us safe this night, Se - cure from all our fears;
4. And when we ear - ly rise And view un - wea - ried sun,

Oh, may we all re - mem-ber well The night of death draws near.
So death will soon dis - robe us all of what we now pos - sess.
May an - gels guard us while we sleep 'Til morn - ing light ap - pears.
May we set out to win the prize And af - ter glo - ry run.

In memory of my brother, Mr. Lafayette S. Cleveland

I Will Trust in the Lord

Traditional

Traditional
Arr. by J. Jefferson Cleveland, 1937-

Slowly, but very rhythmic

1. I will trust in the Lord, I will trust in the Lord,
2. Sis-ter, will you trust in the Lord, Sis-ter, will you trust in the Lord,

I will trust in the Lord 'til I die.
Sis-ter, will you trust in the Lord 'til you die?

I will trust in the Lord, I will trust in the Lord,
Sis-ter, will you trust in the Lord, Sis-ter, will you trust in the Lord?

I will trust in the Lord 'til I die.
Sis-ter, will you trust in the Lord 'til you die?

Other verses may be used:
3. Brother, will you trust . . 4. Deacon, will you trust . . 5. Preacher, will you trust . .

When We All Get to Heaven

15

Eliza Edmunds Hewitt, 1851-1920

Emily Divine Wilson, 1865-1942

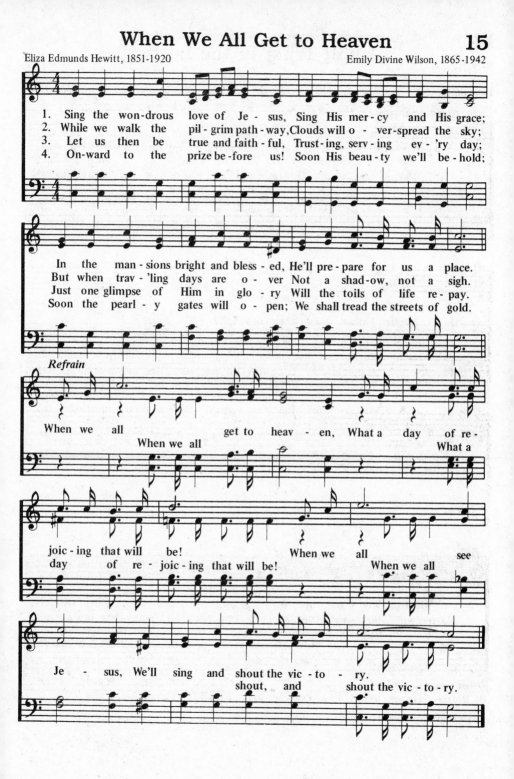

1. Sing the won-drous love of Je - sus, Sing His mer - cy and His grace;
2. While we walk the pil - grim path - way, Clouds will o - ver-spread the sky;
3. Let us then be true and faith - ful, Trust-ing, serv - ing ev - 'ry day;
4. On-ward to the prize be -fore us! Soon His beau - ty we'll be - hold;

In the man - sions bright and bless - ed, He'll pre - pare for us a place.
But when trav - 'ling days are o - ver Not a shad-ow, not a sigh.
Just one glimpse of Him in glo - ry Will the toils of life re - pay.
Soon the pearl - y gates will o - pen; We shall tread the streets of gold.

Refrain

When we all get to heav - en, What a day of re -

When we all

What a

joic - ing that will be! When we all see

day of re - joic - ing that will be! When we all

Je - sus, We'll sing and shout the vic - to - ry.

shout, and shout the vic - to - ry.

16 It's Real

H. L. C.

H. L. Cox

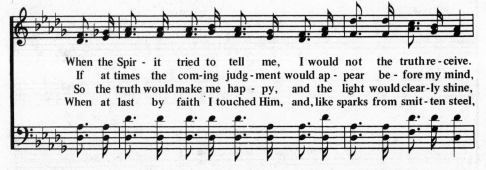

1. O how well do I re-mem-ber how I doubt-ed day by day.
2. When the truth came close and search-ing, all my joy would dis-ap-pear.
3. But at last I tired of liv-ing such a life of fear and doubt.
4. So I prayed to God in ear-nest, and not car-ing what folks said.

For I did not know for cer-tain that my sins were washed a-way;
For I did not have the wit-ness of the Spir-it bright and clear;
For I want-ed God to give me some-thing I would know a-bout;
I was hun-gry for the bless-ing; my poor soul it must be fed;

When the Spir-it tried to tell me, I would not the truth re-ceive.
If at times the com-ing judg-ment would ap-pear be-fore my mind,
So the truth would make me hap-py, and the light would clear-ly shine,
When at last by faith I touched Him, and, like sparks from smit-ten steel,

I en-deav-ored to be hap-py, and to make my-self be-lieve.
O it made me so un - eas - y, for God's smile I could not find.
And the Spir - it gave as - sur - ance that I'm His and He is mine.
Just so quick sal - va - tion reached me; O bless God, I know it's real!

Refrain

But it's real,   it's real   it's real, O I know   it's real;
          it's real   I know

Praise God, the doubts are set - tled, For   I   know, I know it's real.

17 # Jesus Loves Me

Anna Warner, 1820-1915

William B. Bradbury, 1816-1868

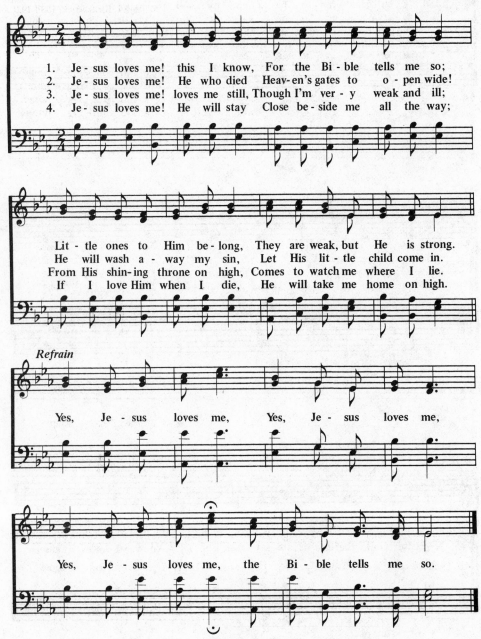

1. Je - sus loves me! this I know, For the Bi - ble tells me so;
2. Je - sus loves me! He who died Heav-en's gates to o - pen wide!
3. Je - sus loves me! loves me still, Though I'm ver - y weak and ill;
4. Je - sus loves me! He will stay Close be - side me all the way;

Lit - tle ones to Him be - long, They are weak, but He is strong.
He will wash a - way my sin, Let His lit - tle child come in.
From His shin-ing throne on high, Comes to watch me where I lie.
If I love Him when I die, He will take me home on high.

Refrain

Yes, Je - sus loves me, Yes, Je - sus loves me,

Yes, Je - sus loves me, the Bi - ble tells me so.

Lord, I'm Coming Home

W. J. K.

COMING HOME
William J. Kirkpatrick, 1838-1921

1. I've wan-dered far a - way from God — Now I'm com - ing home;
2. I've wast-ed man - y pre - cious years — Now I'm com - ing home;
3. I've tired of sin and stray - ing, Lord — Now I'm com - ing home;
4. My soul is sick, my heart is sore — Now I'm com - ing home;

The paths of sin too long I've trod – Lord, I'm com -ing home.
I now re - pent with bit - ter tears – Lord, I'm com -ing home.
I'll trust Thy love, be - lieve Thy word –Lord, I'm com -ing home.
My strength re - new, my hope re - store –Lord, I'm com -ing home.

Refrain

Com - ing home, com - ing home, Nev - er more to roam;

O - pen wide Thine arms of love — Lord, I'm com - ing home.

19   Jesus, Keep Me Near the Cross

William H. Doane, 1832-1915
Harm. by J. Jefferson Cleveland, 1937-
and Verolga Nix, 1933-

Fanny J. Crosby, 1820-1915

1. Je - sus, keep me near the cross; There's a pre - cious foun - tain,
2. Near the cross, a trem - bling soul, Love and mer - cy found me;
3. Near the cross! O Lamb of God, Bring its scenes be - fore me;
4. Near the cross I'll watch and wait, Hop - ing, trust - ing ev - er,

Free to all, a heal - ing stream, Flows from Cal - v'ry's moun - tain.
There the bright and morn - ing star Sheds its beams a - round me.
Help me walk from day to day With its shad - ows o'er me.
Till I reach the gold - en strand Just be - yond the riv - er.

Refrain

In the cross, in the cross, Be my glo - ry ev - er,

Till my rap - tured soul shall find Rest be - yond the riv - er.

It Is Well with My Soul

Horatio G. Spafford, 1828-1888

VILLE DU HAVRE
P. P. Bliss, 1838-1876

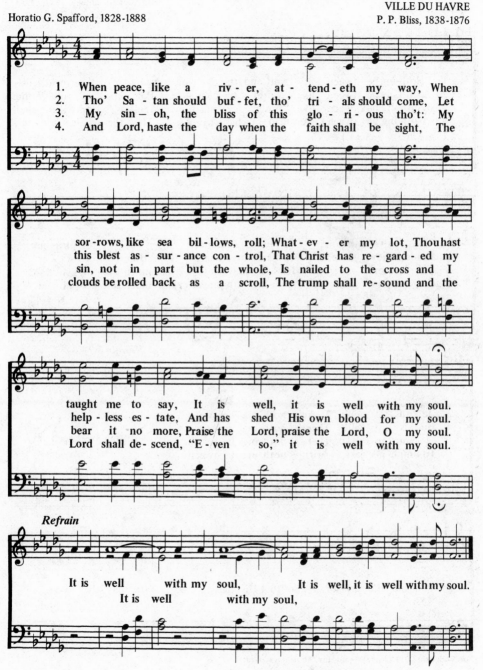

1. When peace, like a riv-er, at-tend-eth my way, When sor-rows, like sea bil-lows, roll; What-ev-er my lot, Thou hast taught me to say, It is well, it is well with my soul.

2. Tho' Sa-tan should buf-fet, tho' tri-als should come, Let this blest as-sur-ance con-trol, That Christ has re-gard-ed my help-less es-tate, And has shed His own blood for my soul.

3. My sin — oh, the bliss of this glo-ri-ous tho't: My sin, not in part but the whole, Is nailed to the cross and I bear it no more, Praise the Lord, praise the Lord, O my soul.

4. And Lord, haste the day when the faith shall be sight, The clouds be rolled back as a scroll, The trump shall re-sound and the Lord shall de-scend, "E-ven so," it is well with my soul.

Refrain

It is well with my soul, It is well, it is well with my soul.
It is well with my soul,

21

Nothing Between

Charles A. Tindley, 1851 - 1933
Arr. by J. Edward Hoy, 1920 -

C.A.T.

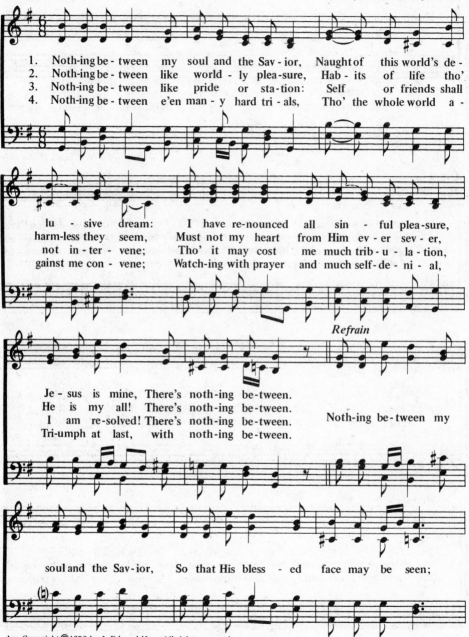

1. Noth-ing be - tween my soul and the Sav - ior, Naught of this world's de -
2. Noth-ing be - tween like world - ly plea-sure, Hab - its of life tho'
3. Noth-ing be - tween like pride or sta - tion: Self or friends shall
4. Noth-ing be - tween e'en man - y hard tri - als, Tho' the whole world a -

lu - sive dream: I have re-nounced all sin - ful plea-sure,
harm-less they seem, Must not my heart from Him ev - er sev - er,
not in - ter - vene; Tho' it may cost me much trib - u - la - tion,
gainst me con - vene; Watch-ing with prayer and much self-de - ni - al,

Refrain

Je - sus is mine, There's noth-ing be-tween.
He is my all! There's noth-ing be-tween.
I am re-solved! There's noth-ing be-tween.
Tri-umph at last, with noth-ing be-tween.

Noth-ing be - tween my

soul and the Sav - ior, So that His bless - ed face may be seen;

Arr. Copyright ©1979 by J. Edward Hoy. All rights reserved.

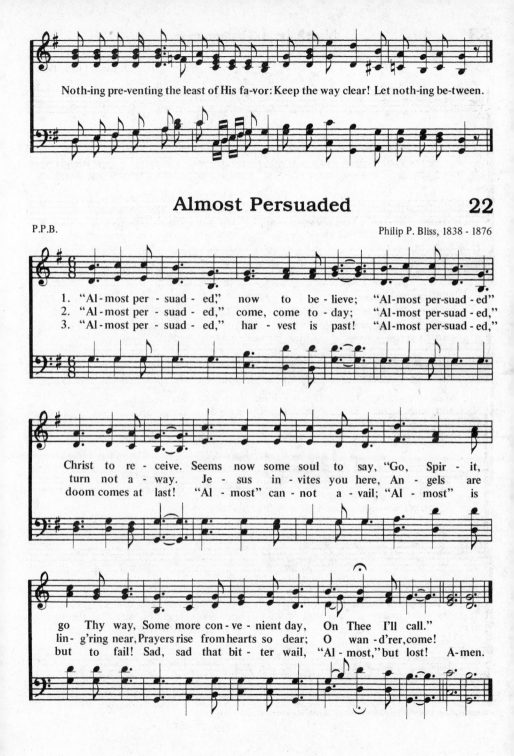

Noth-ing pre-venting the least of His fa-vor: Keep the way clear! Let noth-ing be-tween.

Almost Persuaded

22

P.P.B.

Philip P. Bliss, 1838 - 1876

1. "Al-most per - suad - ed," now to be - lieve; "Al-most per-suad - ed"
2. "Al-most per - suad - ed," come, come to - day; "Al-most per-suad - ed,"
3. "Al-most per - suad - ed," har - vest is past! "Al-most per-suad - ed,"

Christ to re - ceive. Seems now some soul to say, "Go, Spir - it,
turn not a - way. Je - sus in - vites you here, An - gels are
doom comes at last! "Al - most" can - not a - vail; "Al - most" is

go Thy way, Some more con - ve - nient day, On Thee I'll call."
lin- g'ring near, Prayers rise from hearts so dear; O wan - d'rer, come!
but to fail! Sad, sad that bit - ter wail, "Al - most," but lost! A-men.

23 Leave It There

Charles A. Tindley, 1851-1933
C A.T.
Arr. by Verolga Nix, 1933-

Lively

1. If the world from you with-hold, of its sil - ver and its gold,
2. If your bod - y suf - fers pain, and your health you can't re - gain,
3. When your en - e - mies as - sail, and your heart be - gins to fail,
4. When your youth-ful days are gone, and old age is steal-ing on,

And you have to get a - long with mea - ger fare,
And your soul is al - most sink - ing in de - spair,
Don't for - get that God in heav - en an - swers prayer;
And your bod - y bends be - neath the weight of care,

Just re - mem - ber in His word, How He feeds the lit - tle bird,
Je - sus knows the pain you feel, He can save and He can heal,
He will make a way for you, and will lead you safe - ly through,
He will nev - er leave you then, He'll go with you to the end,

Take your bur-den to the Lord and leave it there.
Take your bur-den to the Lord and leave it there.
Take your bur-den to the Lord and leave it there.
Take your bur-den to the Lord and leave it there. (leave it there.)

Refrain

Leave it there, leave it there,
leave it there, leave it there,

Take your bur-den to the Lord and leave it there.
leave it there.

If you trust and nev-er doubt, He will sure-ly bring you out;

Take your bur-den to the Lord and leave it there.
leave it there.

24 Battle Hymn of the Republic

Julia Ward Howe, 1819-1910

BATTLE HYMN OF THE REPUBLIC
American Camp Meeting Tune

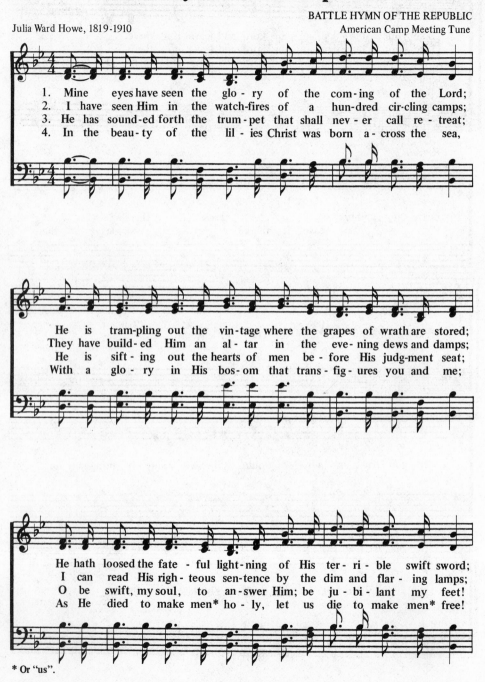

1. Mine eyes have seen the glo-ry of the com-ing of the Lord;
2. I have seen Him in the watch-fires of a hun-dred cir-cling camps;
3. He has sound-ed forth the trum-pet that shall nev-er call re-treat;
4. In the beau-ty of the lil-ies Christ was born a-cross the sea,

He is tram-pling out the vin-tage where the grapes of wrath are stored;
They have build-ed Him an al-tar in the eve-ning dews and damps;
He is sift-ing out the hearts of men be-fore His judg-ment seat;
With a glo-ry in His bos-om that trans-fig-ures you and me;

He hath loosed the fate-ful light-ning of His ter-ri-ble swift sword;
I can read His righ-teous sen-tence by the dim and flar-ing lamps;
O be swift, my soul, to an-swer Him; be ju-bi-lant my feet!
As He died to make men* ho-ly, let us die to make men* free!

* Or "us".

Refrain

His truth is march-ing on.
His day is march-ing on.
Our God is march-ing on.
While God is march-ing on.

Glo - ry, glo - ry! Hal - le -

lu - jah! Glo - ry, glo - ry! Hal - le - lu - jah! Glo - ry,

glo - ry! Hal - le - lu - jah! His truth is march - ing on.

25 I'll Overcome Someday

C. A. T.

C. Albert Tindley, 1851-1933

1. This world is one great bat - tle - field, With for - ces all ar - rayed;
2. Both seen and un - seen pow - ers join To drive my soul a - stray,
3. A thou - sand snares are set for me, And moun - tains in my way;
4. I fail so of - ten when I try My Sav - ior to o - bey;
5. My mind is not to do the wrong, But walk the nar - row way;
6. Tho' many a time no signs ap - pear, Of an - swer when I pray;

If in my heart I do not yield I'll o - ver - come some day.
But with God's Word a sword of mine, I'll o - ver - come some day.
If Je - sus will my lead - er be, I'll o - ver - come some day.
It pains my heart and then I cry, Lord, make me strong some day.
I'm pray - ing as I jour - ney on, To o - ver - come some day.
My Je - sus says I need not fear, He'll make it plain some day.

Refrain

I'll o - ver - come some day, I'll o - ver - come some day;
I'll o - ver - come some day, I'll o - ver - come some day;
I'll o - ver - come some day, I'll o - ver - come some day;
Lord, make me strong some day, Lord, make me strong some day;
To o - ver - come some day, To o - ver - come some day;
I'll be like Him some day, I'll be like Him some day;
some day,

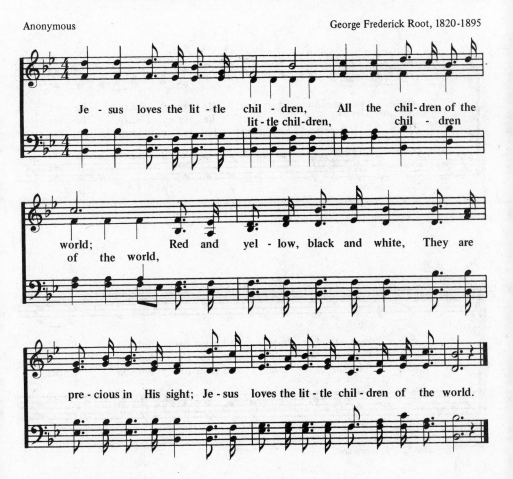

If in my heart I do not yield I'll o-ver-come some day.
But with God's Word a sword of mine, I'll o-ver-come some day.
If Je-sus will my lead-er be, I'll o-ver-come some day.
It pains my heart and then I cry, Lord, make me strong some day.
I'm pray-ing as I jour-ney on, To o-ver-come some day.
My Je-sus says I need not fear, I'll be like Him some day.

Jesus Loves the Little Children 26

Anonymous

George Frederick Root, 1820-1895

Je - sus loves the lit - tle chil - dren, All the chil-dren of the
lit - tle chil-dren, chil - dren

world; Red and yel - low, black and white, They are
of the world,

pre - cious in His sight; Je - sus loves the lit - tle chil - dren of the world.

27 In Times Like These

R. C. J.

Ruth Caye Jones 1902-1972

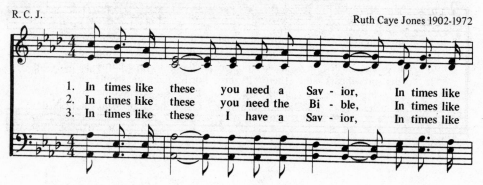

1. In times like these you need a Sav - ior, In times like
2. In times like these you need the Bi - ble, In times like
3. In times like these I have a Sav - ior, In times like

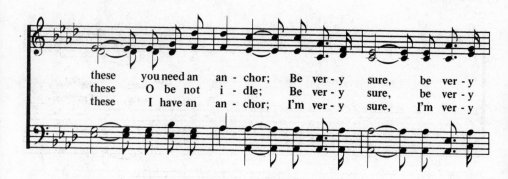

these you need an an - chor; Be ver - y sure, be ver - y
these O be not i - dle; Be ver - y sure, be ver - y
these I have an an - chor; I'm ver - y sure, I'm ver - y

sure Your an - chor holds and grips the Sol - id Rock!
sure Your an - chor holds and grips the Sol - id Rock!
sure My an - chor holds and grips the Sol - id Rock!

Refrain

This Rock is Je - sus, Yes, He's the One; This Rock is
Je - sus, The on - ly One! 1.,2. Be ver - y sure, be ver - y
3. I'm ver - y sure, I'm ver - y

sure Your an - chor holds and grips the Sol - id Rock!
sure My an - chor holds and grips the Sol - id Rock!

28 Farther Along

W. B. S.

W. B. Stevens
Arr. J. R. Baxter, Jr.

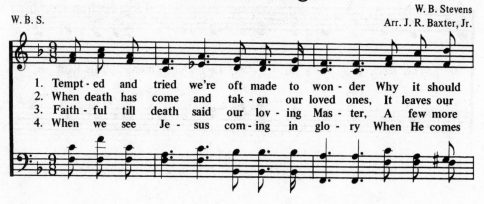

1. Tempt-ed and tried we're oft made to won-der Why it should
2. When death has come and tak-en our loved ones, It leaves our
3. Faith-ful till death said our lov-ing Mas-ter, A few more
4. When we see Je-sus com-ing in glo-ry When He comes

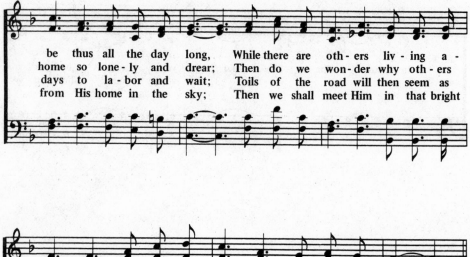

be thus all the day long, While there are oth-ers liv-ing a-
home so lone-ly and drear; Then do we won-der why oth-ers
days to la-bor and wait; Toils of the road will then seem as
from His home in the sky; Then we shall meet Him in that bright

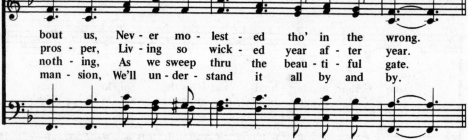

bout us, Nev-er mo-lest-ed tho' in the wrong.
pros-per, Liv-ing so wick-ed year af-ter year.
noth-ing, As we sweep thru the beau-ti-ful gate.
man-sion, We'll un-der-stand it all by and by.

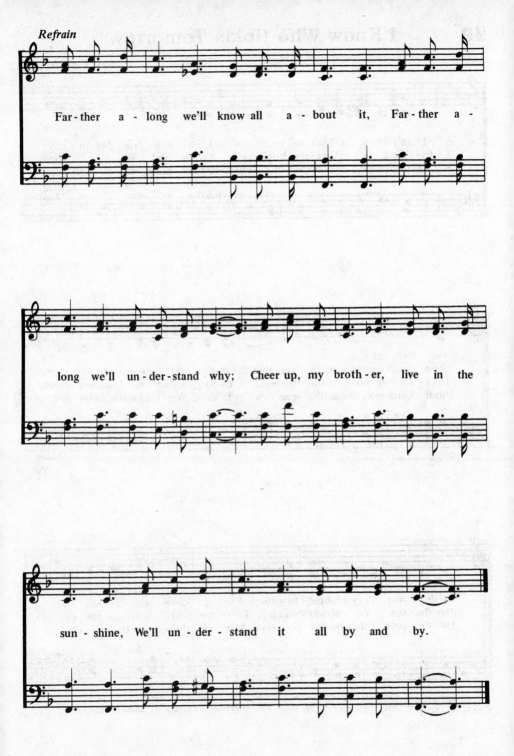

Far - ther a - long we'll know all a - bout it, Far - ther a -

long we'll un - der - stand why; Cheer up, my broth - er, live in the

sun - shine, We'll un - der - stand it all by and by.

29 I Know Who Holds Tomorrow

I. F. S.

Ira F. Stanphill, 1914-

1. I don't know a-bout to-mor-row, I just live from day to day.
2. Ev-'ry step is get-ting bright-er, As the gold-en stairs I climb;
3. I don't know a-bout to-mor-row, It may bring me pov-er-ty;

I don't bor-row from its sun-shine, For its skies may turn to gray.
Ev-'ry bur-den's get-ting light-er; Ev-'ry cloud is sil-ver lined.
But the one who feeds the spar-row, Is the one who stands by me.

I don't wor-ry o'er the fu-ture, For I know what Je-sus said,
There the sun is al-ways shin-ing, There no tear will dim the eye,
And the path that be my por-tion, May be through the flame or flood,

And to - day I'll walk be - side Him, For He knows what is a - head.
At the end - ing of the rain - bow, Where the moun - tains touch the sky.
But His pres - ence goes be - fore me, And I'm cov - ered with His blood.

Refrain

Man - y things a - bout to - mor - row, I don't seem to un - der - stand;

But I know who holds to - mor - row, And I know who holds my hand.

30 He Lives

A. H. A.

Alfred H. Ackley, 1887-1960

1. I serve a ris - en Sav - ior, He's in the world to - day;
2. In all the world a - round me I see His lov - ing care,
3. Re - joice, re - joice. O Chris - tian, lift up your voice and sing

I know that He is liv - ing, what - ev - er men* may say;
And tho' my heart grows wea - ry I nev - er will de - spair;
E - ter - nal hal - le - lu - jahs to Je - sus Christ, the King!

I see His hand of mer - cy, I hear His voice of cheer,
I know that He is lead - ing through all the storm - y blast,
The hope of all who seek Him, the help of all who find,

And just the time I need Him He's al - ways near.
The day of His ap - pear - ing will come at last.
None oth - er is so lov - ing, so good and kind.

*"oth-ers" may be substituted for "men may."

Refrain

He lives, He lives, Christ Je - sus lives to - day!
He lives, He lives,

He walks with me and talks with me a - long life's nar - row way.

He lives, He lives, sal - va - tion to im - part!
He lives, He lives,

You ask me how I know He lives? He lives with-in my heart.

He Looked Beyond My Fault

Dottie Rambo

LONDONDERRY
Irish trad. melody

A - maz-ing grace shall al-ways be my song of praise,

For it was grace that bought my lib - er - ty;

I do not know just why He came to love me so,

He looked be - yond my fault and saw my need.

I shall for - ev - er lift mine eyes to Cal - va - ry,

To view the cross where Je - sus died for me;

How mar - vel - ous the grace that caught my fall - ing soul,

He looked be - yond my fault and saw my need.

32   Lift Every Voice and Sing

James Weldon Johnson, 1871 - 1938

J. Rosamond Johnson, 1873 - 1954

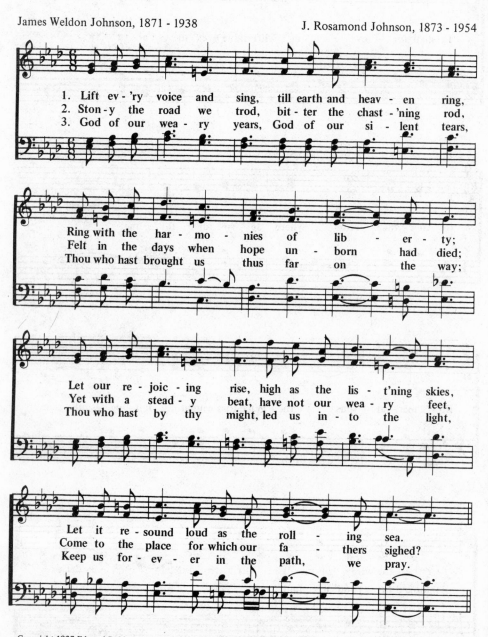

1. Lift ev - 'ry voice and sing, till earth and heav - en ring,
2. Ston - y the road we trod, bit - ter the chast - 'ning rod,
3. God of our wea - ry years, God of our si - lent tears,

Ring with the har - mo - nies of lib - er - ty;
Felt in the days when hope un - born had died;
Thou who hast brought us thus far on the way;

Let our re - joic - ing rise, high as the lis - t'ning skies,
Yet with a stead - y beat, have not our wea - ry feet,
Thou who hast by thy might, led us in - to the light,

Let it re - sound loud as the roll - ing sea.
Come to the place for which our fa - thers sighed?
Keep us for - ev - er in the path, we pray.

Sing a song full of the faith that the dark past has taught us,
We have come o-ver a way that with tears has been wa-tered,
Lest our feet stray from the plac-es, our God, where we met Thee,

Sing a song full of the hope that the pres-ent has brought us;
We have come, tread-ing our path thro' the blood of the slaugh-tered,
Lest our hearts, drunk with the wine of the world, we for-get Thee;

ff

Fac-ing the ris-ing sun of our new day be-gun,
Out from the gloom-y past, till now we stand at last
Shad-owed be-neath Thy hand, May we for-ev-er stand,

Let us march on till vic-to-ry is won.
Where the white gleam of our bright star is cast.
True to our God, true to our na-tive land.

33 His Eye Is on the Sparrow

Civilla D. Martin, 1860-1948

Charles H. Gabriel, 1856-1932

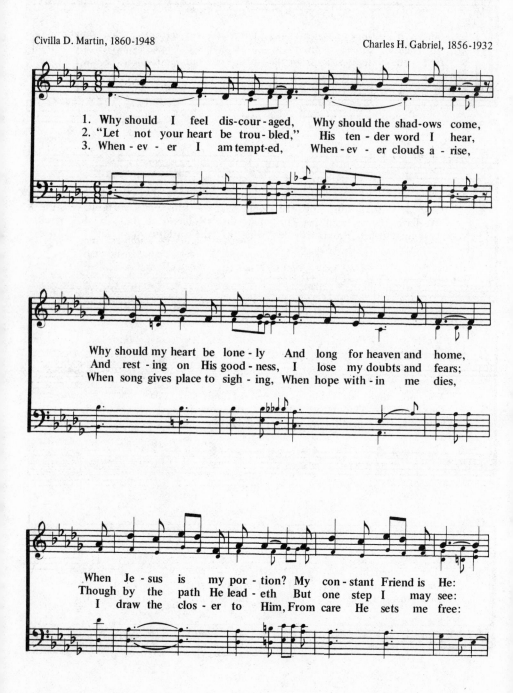

34   Is Your All on the Altar?

E. A. H.

Elisha A. Hoffman, 1839-1929

1. You have longed for sweet peace and for faith to in - crease,
2. Would you walk with the Lord in the light of His Word,
3. O we nev - er can know what the Lord will be - stow
4. Who can tell all the love He will send from a - bove,

And have ear-nest-ly, fer-vent-ly prayed; But you can-not have
And have peace and con - tent-ment al - way? You must do His sweet
Of the bless-ings for which we have prayed Till our bod - y and
And how hap-py our hearts will be made; Of the fel - low-ship

rest or be per-fect-ly blest Un-til all on the al-tar is laid.
will to be free from all ill, On the al-tar your all you must lay.
soul He doth ful - ly con-trol, And our all on the al-tar is laid.
sweet we shall share at His feet When our all on the al-tar is laid.

Refrain

Is your all on the al - tar of sac - ri - fice laid?

Your heart does the Spir - it con - trol? You can on - ly be blest

and have peace and sweet rest As you yield Him your bod - y and soul.

35 I Shall Not Be Moved

Traditional
Arr. by J. Jefferson Cleveland, 1937-
and Verolga Nix, 1933-

Traditional

Spirited

1. I shall not,
2. Je-sus is my cap-tain,
3. On my way to glo - ry,

I shall not be moved. I shall not,
I shall not be moved. Je-sus is my cap-tain, I shall not be moved, just like a
I shall not be moved. On my way to glo-ry,

tree that's plant-ed by the wa - ter I shall not be moved.

Other verses may be used:
4. I'm climbing Jacob's ladder . . .   5. Old Satan tried to stop me . . .

Arr. copyright © 1981 by Abingdon.

Oh, How I Love Jesus

Frederick Whitfield, 1829-1904

Traditional

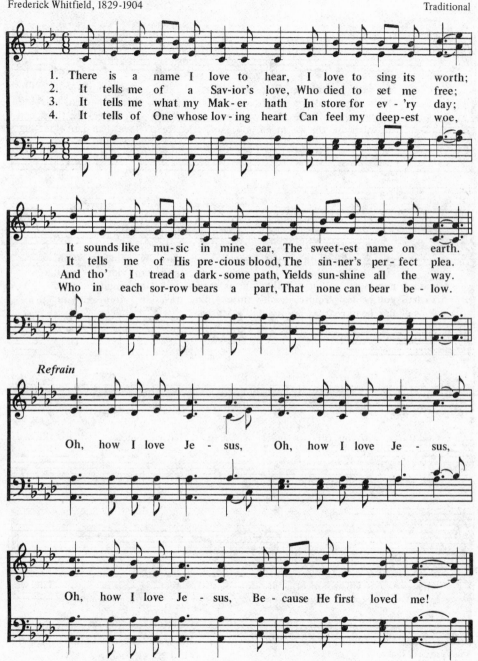

1. There is a name I love to hear, I love to sing its worth;
2. It tells me of a Sav-ior's love, Who died to set me free;
3. It tells me what my Mak-er hath In store for ev-'ry day;
4. It tells of One whose lov-ing heart Can feel my deep-est woe,

It sounds like mu-sic in mine ear, The sweet-est name on earth.
It tells me of His pre-cious blood, The sin-ner's per-fect plea.
And tho' I tread a dark-some path, Yields sun-shine all the way.
Who in each sor-row bears a part, That none can bear be-low.

Refrain

Oh, how I love Je - sus, Oh, how I love Je - sus,

Oh, how I love Je - sus, Be - cause He first loved me!

God Be with You

Jeremiah E. Rankin, 1828-1904

William G. Tomer, 1832-1896

1. God be with you till we meet a - gain; By His coun-sels guide, up -
2. God be with you till we meet a - gain; 'Neath His wings pro - tect - ing
3. God be with you till we meet a - gain; When life's per - ils thick con -
4. God be with you till we meet a - gain; Keep love's ban - ner float - ing

hold you, With His sheep se - cure - ly fold you:
hide you, Dai - ly man - na still pro - vide you:
found you, Put * His arms un - fail - ing round you:
o'er you, Smite death's threat -'ning wave be - fore you:

Refrain

God be with you till we meet a - gain. Till we meet, till we

meet, Till we meet at Je - sus' feet, Till we
till we meet,

* or, warm

meet,   till we meet   God be with you till we meet a - gain.

No, Not One!   38

HARPER MEMORIAL

Johnson Oatman, Jr. 1856-1922   George C. Hugg, 1848-1907

1. There's not   a   friend   like the   low - ly   Je - sus — No, not one!   No, not one!
2.   No friend like Him   is   so   high and ho - ly — No, not one!   No, not one!
3. There's not   an   hour   that He   is   not near us — No, not one!   No, not one!
4.   Did   ev - er   saint   find this Friend for-sake Him? No, not one!   No, not one!
5.   Was   e'er   a   gift   like the   Sav - ior giv - en?   No, not one!   No, not one!

Fine

None else could heal   all our soul's dis - eas - es — No, not one!   No, not one!
And   yet, no   friend   is   so meek and low - ly — No, not one!   No, not one!
No night so   dark but His   love can cheer us — No, not one!   No, not one!
Or   sin - ner   find   that He would not take him? No, not one!   No, not one!
Will   He   re - fuse   us   a   home in heav - en?   No, not one!   No, not one!

D.S.—There's not   a   friend   like the   low - ly   Je - sus — No, not one!   no, not one!

Refrain   *D.S.*

Je - sus knows all   a - bout our strug-gles,   He will guide till the day is done;

39 Higher Ground

Johnson Oatman, Jr., 1856-1922

HIGHER GROUND
Charles H. Gabriel, 1856-1932

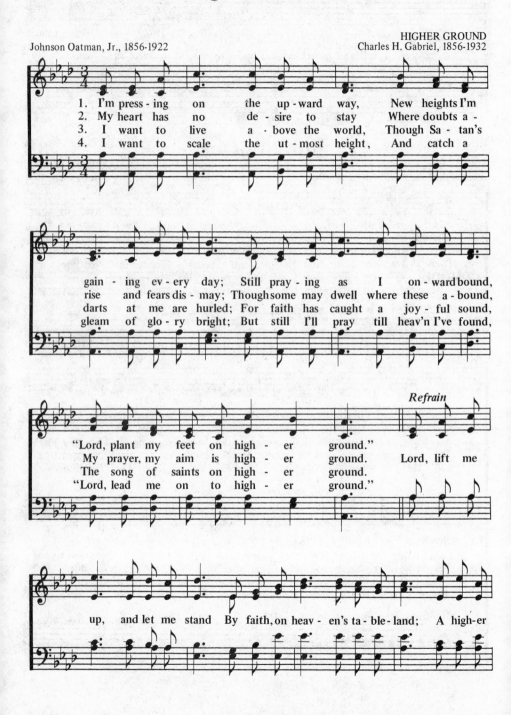

1. I'm press-ing on the up-ward way, New heights I'm
2. My heart has no de-sire to stay Where doubts a-
3. I want to live a-bove the world, Though Sa-tan's
4. I want to scale the ut-most height, And catch a

gain-ing ev-ery day; Still pray-ing as I on-ward bound,
rise and fears dis-may; Though some may dwell where these a-bound,
darts at me are hurled; For faith has caught a joy-ful sound,
gleam of glo-ry bright; But still I'll pray till heav'n I've found,

Refrain

"Lord, plant my feet on high-er ground."
My prayer, my aim is high-er ground. Lord, lift me
The song of saints on high-er ground.
"Lord, lead me on to high-er ground."

up, and let me stand By faith, on heav-en's ta-ble-land; A high-er

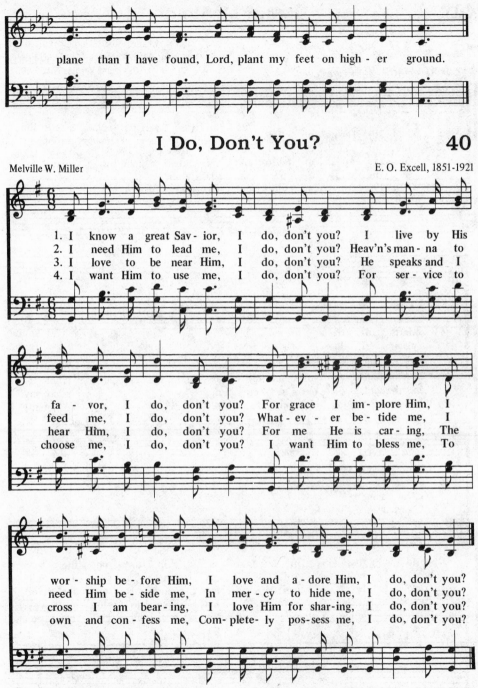

plane than I have found, Lord, plant my feet on high - er ground.

I Do, Don't You?   40

Melville W. Miller

E. O. Excell, 1851-1921

1. I know a great Sav - ior, I do, don't you? I live by His
2. I need Him to lead me, I do, don't you? Heav'n's man - na to
3. I love to be near Him, I do, don't you? He speaks and I
4. I want Him to use me, I do, don't you? For ser - vice to

fa - vor, I do, don't you? For grace I im - plore Him, I
feed me, I do, don't you? What - ev - er be - tide me, I
hear Him, I do, don't you? For me He is car - ing, The
choose me, I do, don't you? I want Him to bless me, To

wor - ship be - fore Him, I love and a - dore Him, I do, don't you?
need Him be - side me, In mer - cy to hide me, I do, don't you?
cross I am bear - ing, I love Him for shar - ing, I do, don't you?
own and con - fess me, Com - plete - ly pos - sess me, I do, don't you?

41 Stand by Me

Charles Albert Tindley,1851-1933
Arr. by J. Jefferson Cleveland, 1937-
and Verolga Nix, 1933-

C. A. T.

Reverently - Moderate speed

1. When the storms of life are rag - ing,
2. In the midst of trib - u - la - tion,
3. In the midst of faults and fail - ures, Stand by me;
4. In the midst of per - se - cu - tion,
5. When I'm grow - ing old and fee - ble,

When the storms of life are rag - ing, When the
In the midst of trib - u - la - tion, When the
In the midst of faults and fail - ures, Stand by me. When I
In the midst of per - se - cu - tion, When my
When I'm grow - ing old and fee - ble, When my

world is toss - ing me, Like a ship up - on the sea;
hosts of hell as - sail, And my strength be - gins to fail,
do the best I can, And my friends mis - un - der - stand,
foes in bat - tle ar - ray Un - der - take to stop my way,
life be - comes a bur - den, And I'm near - ing chil - ly Jor - dan,

Thou who rul - est wind and wa - ter,
Thou who nev - er lost a bat - tle,
Thou who know - est all a - bout me, Stand by me.
Thou who sav - ed Paul and Si - las,
O Thou "Lil - y of the Val - ley,"

Where He Leads Me 42

E. W. Blandy

John Samuel Norris, 1844-1907

1. I can hear my Sav - ior call - ing, I can hear my Sav - ior call - ing,
2. I'll go with Him thru the gar - den, I'll go with Him thru the gar - den,
3. I'll go with Him thru the judg - ment, I'll go with Him thru the judg - ment,
4. He will give me grace and glo - ry, He will give me grace and glo - ry,

Refrain—Where He leads me I will fol - low, Where He leads me I will fol - low,

I can hear my Sav - ior call - ing, "Take thy cross and fol - low, fol - low Me."
I'll go with Him thru the gar - den, I'll go with Him, with Him all the way.
I'll go with Him thru the judg - ment, I'll go with Him, with Him all the way.
He will give me grace and glo - ry, And go with me, with me all the way.
Where He leads me I will fol - low,—I'll go with Him, with Him all the way.

Where He leads me I will fol - low, I'll go with Him, with Him all the way.

43 I Believe It

C. A. T., Sr.

Charles Albert Tindley, 1851-1933
Arr. by Charles A. Tindley, Jr.

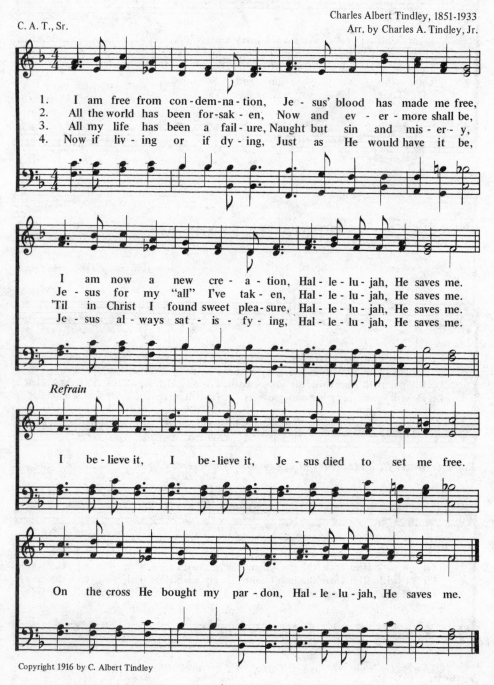

1. I am free from con-dem-na-tion, Je - sus' blood has made me free,
2. All the world has been for-sak - en, Now and ev - er - more shall be,
3. All my life has been a fail-ure, Naught but sin and mis-er - y,
4. Now if liv - ing or if dy - ing, Just as He would have it be,

I am now a new cre - a - tion, Hal - le - lu - jah, He saves me.
Je - sus for my "all" I've tak - en, Hal - le - lu - jah, He saves me.
'Til in Christ I found sweet plea- sure, Hal - le - lu - jah, He saves me.
Je - sus al - ways sat - is - fy - ing, Hal - le - lu - jah, He saves me.

Refrain

I be - lieve it, I be - lieve it, Je - sus died to set me free.

On the cross He bought my par - don, Hal - le - lu - jah, He saves me.

In the Garden

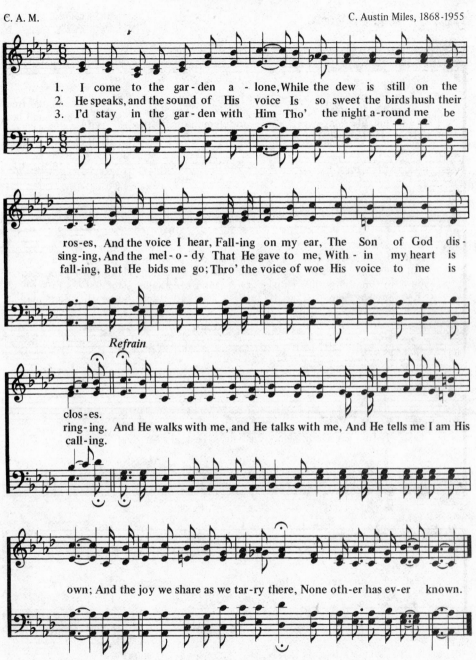

44

C. A. M.

C. Austin Miles, 1868-1955

1. I come to the gar-den a-lone, While the dew is still on the
2. He speaks, and the sound of His voice Is so sweet the birds hush their
3. I'd stay in the gar-den with Him Tho' the night a-round me be

ros-es, And the voice I hear, Fall-ing on my ear, The Son of God dis-
sing-ing, And the mel-o-dy That He gave to me, With-in my heart is
fall-ing, But He bids me go; Thro' the voice of woe His voice to me is

Refrain

clos-es.
ring-ing. And He walks with me, and He talks with me, And He tells me I am His
call-ing.

own; And the joy we share as we tar-ry there, None oth-er has ev-er known.

Lead Me to Calvary

Jennie Evelyn Hussey, 1874-1958

Willaim J. Kirkpatrick, 1838-1921

1. King of my life I crown Thee now—Thine shall the glo - ry be;
2. Show me the tomb where Thou wast laid, Ten - der - ly mourned and wept;
3. Let me, like Ma - ry, thru the gloom, Come with a gift to Thee;
4. May I be will - ing, Lord, to bear Dai - ly my cross for Thee;

Lest I for - get Thy thorn-crowned brow, Lead me to Cal - va - ry.
An - gels in robes of light ar - rayed Guard-ed Thee whilst Thou slept.
Show to me now the emp - ty tomb—Lead me to Cal - va - ry.
E - ven Thy cup of grief to share - Thou hast borne all for me.

Refrain

Lest I for - get Geth - sem - a - ne, Lest I for - get Thine ag - o - ny,

Lest I for - get Thy love for me, Lead me to Cal - va - ry.

Just a Closer Walk with Thee

Traditional

Traditional

Slow for solo, spiritually for chorus

Refrain

Just a clos-er walk with Thee; Grant it, Je-sus, if you please,

Dai-ly walk-ing close with Thee, Let it be, dear Lord, let it be.

Fine

Verses

1. I am weak but Thou art strong, Je-sus, keep me from all wrong,
2. Through this world of toils and snares, If I fal-ter, Lord, who cares?
3. When my fee-ble life is o'er, Time for me won't be no more,

D.C.

I'll be sat-is-fied as long, as I walk, Let me walk close with Thee.
Who with me my bur-dens shares? None but Thee, dear Lord, none but Thee.
Guide me gent-ly, safe-ly o'er, To Thy king-dom shore, to Thy shore.

47 Let Jesus Fix It for You

C. A. T.

Charles Albert Tindley, 1851-1933
Arr. by Frederick J. Tindley

1. If your life in days gone by, Has not been good and true,
2. Per-haps your tem-per is to blame, For man-y wrongs you do,
3. If in your home the trou-ble is, The course you should pur-sue,
4. And if some sin your soul hath bound With cords you can't un-do,
5. May-be to you the world is dark, And com-forts far and few,

In your own way no long-er try, But let Him fix it for you.
Take it to God in Je-sus' name, And He will fix it for you.
Go talk with God, your hand in His, And He will fix it for you.
At Je-sus' feet go lay it down, And He will fix it for you.
Let Je-sus own and rule your heart, And He will fix it for you.

Refrain

Let Je-sus fix it for you, He knows just what to do;

rit.

When-ev-er you pray, let Him have His way, And He will fix it for you.

W. C. Martin

Edmund S. Lorenz, 1854-1942

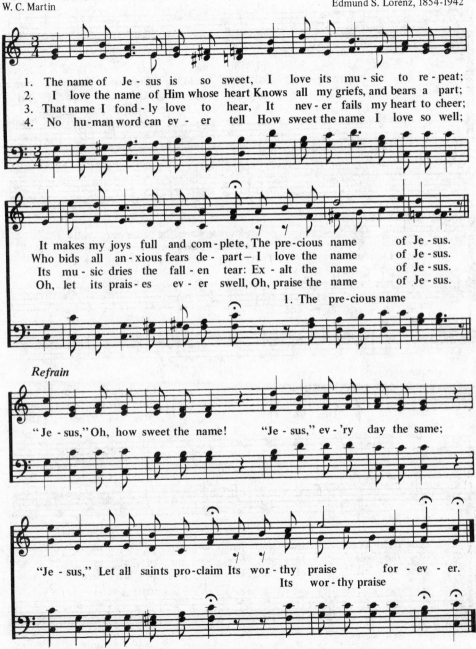

1. The name of Je - sus is so sweet, I love its mu - sic to re - peat;
2. I love the name of Him whose heart Knows all my griefs, and bears a part;
3. That name I fond - ly love to hear, It nev - er fails my heart to cheer;
4. No hu - man word can ev - er tell How sweet the name I love so well;

It makes my joys full and com - plete, The pre - cious name of Je - sus.
Who bids all an - xious fears de - part — I love the name of Je - sus.
Its mu - sic dries the fall - en tear: Ex - alt the name of Je - sus.
Oh, let its prais - es ev - er swell, Oh, praise the name of Je - sus.

1. The pre - cious name

Refrain

"Je - sus," Oh, how sweet the name! "Je - sus," ev - 'ry day the same;

"Je - sus," Let all saints pro - claim Its wor - thy praise for - ev - er.

Its wor - thy praise

49 Jesus, Savior, Pilot Me

Edward Hopper, 1816-1888

John E. Gould, 1822-1875
Arr. by Verolga Nix, 1933-

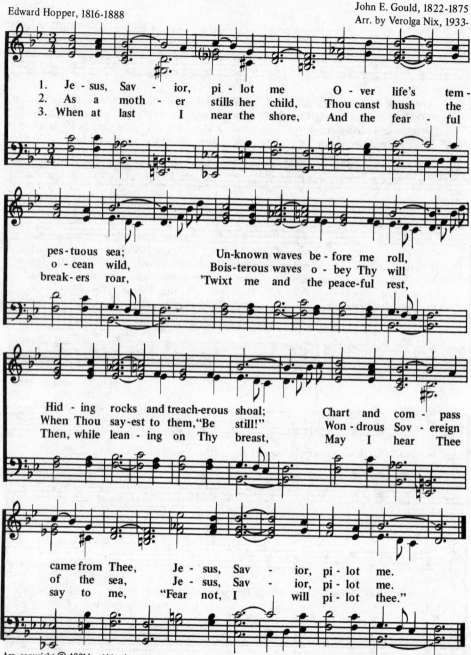

1. Je - sus, Sav - ior, pi - lot me O - ver life's tem -
2. As a moth - er stills her child, Thou canst hush the
3. When at last I near the shore, And the fear - ful

pes - tuous sea; Un-known waves be - fore me roll,
o - cean wild, Bois-terous waves o - bey Thy will
break - ers roar, 'Twixt me and the peace-ful rest,

Hid - ing rocks and treach-erous shoal; Chart and com - pass
When Thou say-est to them, "Be still!" Won - drous Sov - ereign
Then, while lean - ing on Thy breast, May I hear Thee

came from Thee, Je - sus, Sav - ior, pi - lot me.
of the sea, Je - sus, Sav - ior, pi - lot me.
say to me, "Fear not, I will pi - lot thee."

The Right Hand of God

Patrick Prescod

Noel Dexter

1. The right hand of God is writ-ing in our land,
2. The right hand of God is point-ing in' our land,
3. The right hand of God is strik-ing in our land,
4. The right hand of God is heal-ing in our land,
5. The right hand of God is plant-ing in our land,

Writ - ing with pow - er and with love, _____
Point - ing the way we must go. _____
Strik-ing out at en - vy, hate, and greed. _____
Heal-ing bro - ken bod - ies, minds, and souls. _____
Plant-ing seeds of free - dom, hope, and love. _____

Our con - flicts and our fears, our tri - umphs and our
So cloud - ed is the way, so eas - i - ly we
Our sel - fish - ness and lust, our pride and deeds un-
So won - drous is its touch with love that means so
In these Ca - rib - bean lands, let His peo - ple all join

tears Are re - cord-ed by the right hand of God.
stray, But we're guid-ed by the right hand of God.
just Are de - stroyed by the right hand of God.
much, When we're healed by the right hand of God.
hands, And be one with the right hand of God.

51 My Secret of Joy

Charles A. Tindley, 1851-1933
Arr. by William D. Smith

C.A.T.

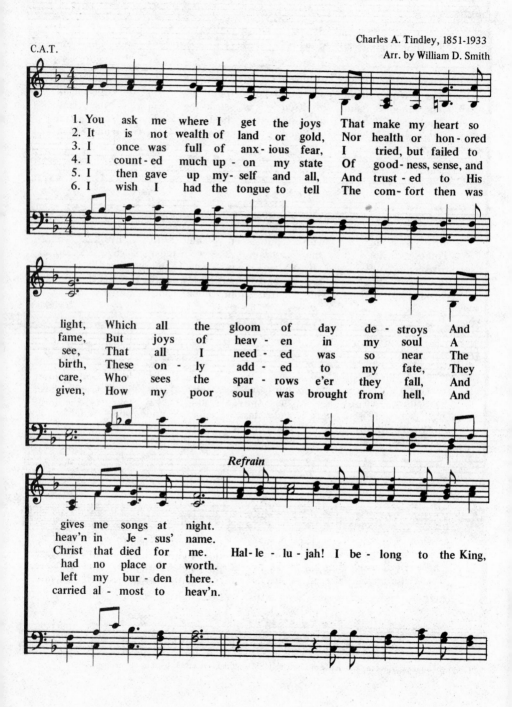

1. You ask me where I get the joys That make my heart so
2. It is not wealth of land or gold, Nor health or hon - ored
3. I once was full of anx - ious fear, I tried, but failed to
4. I count - ed much up - on my state Of good - ness, sense, and
5. I then gave up my - self and all, And trust - ed to His
6. I wish I had the tongue to tell The com - fort then was

light, Which all the gloom of day de - stroys And
fame, But joys of heav - en in my soul A
see, That all I need - ed was so near The
birth, These on - ly add - ed to my fate, They
care, Who sees the spar - rows e'er they fall, And
given, How my poor soul was brought from hell, And

Refrain

gives me songs at night.
heav'n in Je - sus' name.
Christ that died for me.   Hal - le - lu - jah! I be - long to the King,
had no place or worth.
left my bur - den there.
carried al - most to heav'n.

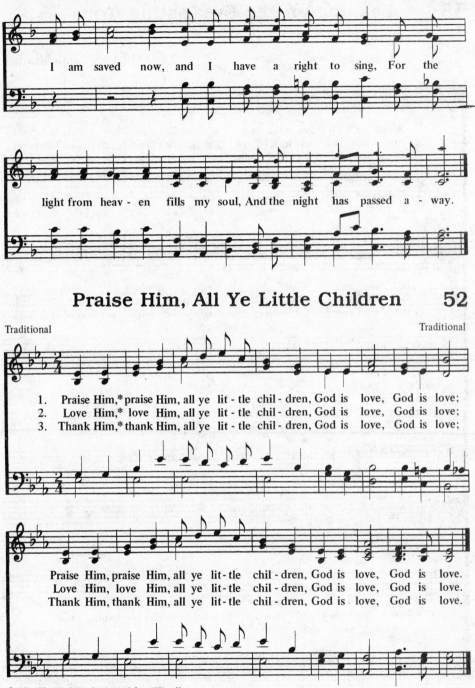

I am saved now, and I have a right to sing, For the light from heav - en fills my soul, And the night has passed a - way.

Praise Him, All Ye Little Children 52

Traditional

Traditional

1. Praise Him,* praise Him, all ye lit - tle chil - dren, God is love, God is love;
2. Love Him,* love Him, all ye lit - tle chil - dren, God is love, God is love;
3. Thank Him,* thank Him, all ye lit - tle chil - dren, God is love, God is love;

Praise Him, praise Him, all ye lit - tle chil - dren, God is love, God is love.
Love Him, love Him, all ye lit - tle chil - dren, God is love, God is love.
Thank Him, thank Him, all ye lit - tle chil - dren, God is love, God is love.

* "God" may be substituted for "Him."

53   Leaning on the Everlasting Arms

Elisha Albright Hoffman, 1839-1929

Anthony Johnson Showalter, 1858-1924

1. What a fel-low-ship, what a joy di-vine, Lean-ing on the ev-er-
2. Oh, how sweet to walk in this pil-grim way, Lean-ing on the ev-er-
3. What have I to dread, what have I to fear, Lean-ing on the ev-er-

last-ing arms; What a bless-ed-ness, what a peace is mine,
last-ing arms; Oh, how bright the path grows from day to day,
last-ing arms? I have bless-ed peace with my Lord so near,

Refrain

Lean-ing on the ev-er-last-ing arms. Lean - ing,
Lean-ing on Je-sus,

lean - ing, Safe and se-cure from all a-larms; Lean -
lean-ing on Je-sus, Lean-ing on

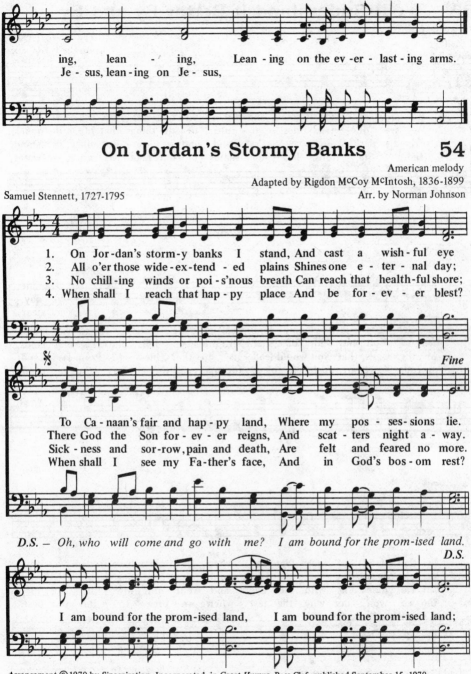

ing, lean - ing, Lean - ing on the ev -er - last - ing arms.
Je - sus, lean - ing on Je - sus,

On Jordan's Stormy Banks 54

American melody
Adapted by Rigdon McCoy McIntosh, 1836-1899
Arr. by Norman Johnson

Samuel Stennett, 1727-1795

1. On Jor-dan's storm-y banks I stand, And cast a wish-ful eye
2. All o'er those wide - ex-tend - ed plains Shines one e - ter - nal day;
3. No chill -ing winds or poi - s'nous breath Can reach that health-ful shore;
4. When shall I reach that hap - py place And be for - ev - er blest?

To Ca - naan's fair and hap - py land, Where my pos - ses - sions lie.
There God the Son for - ev - er reigns, And scat - ters night a - way.
Sick - ness and sor-row, pain and death, Are felt and feared no more.
When shall I see my Fa -ther's face, And in God's bos - om rest?

D.S. — *Oh, who will come and go with me? I am bound for the prom-ised land.*
D.S.

I am bound for the prom-ised land, I am bound for the prom-ised land;

55 We'll Understand It Better By and By

C. A. T.

Charles Albert Tindley, 1851-1933
Arr. by F. A. Clark

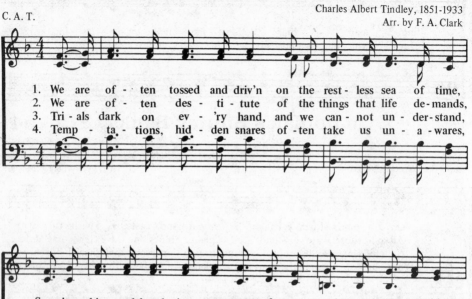

1. We are of - ten tossed and driv'n on the rest - less sea of time,
2. We are of - ten des - ti - tute of the things that life de - mands,
3. Tri - als dark on ev - 'ry hand, and we can - not un - der - stand,
4. Temp - ta - tions, hid - den snares of - ten take us un - a - wares,

Som - ber skies and howl - ing tem - pests oft suc - ceed a bright sun - shine,
Want of food and want of shel - ter, thirst - y hills and bar - ren lands,
All the ways that God would lead us to that bless - ed Prom - ised Land;
And our hearts are made to bleed for many a thought - less word or deed,

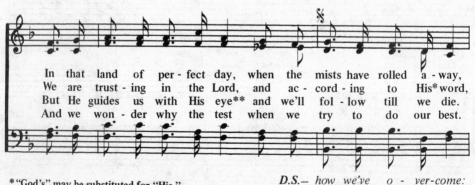

In that land of per - fect day, when the mists have rolled a - way,
We are trust - ing in the Lord, and ac - cord - ing to His* word,
But He guides us with His eye** and we'll fol - low till we die.
And we won - der why the test when we try to do our best.

*"God's" may be substituted for "His."

D.S.— *how we've o - ver-come:*

**"We are guided by God's eye" may be substituted for "But He guides us with His eye."

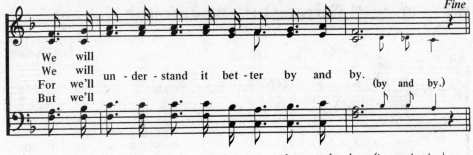

We will
We will un - der - stand it bet - ter by and by.
For we'll   (by and by.)
But we'll

For we'll un - der - stand it bet - ter by and by. (by and by.)

Refrain

By and by when the morn - ing comes, When the saints of

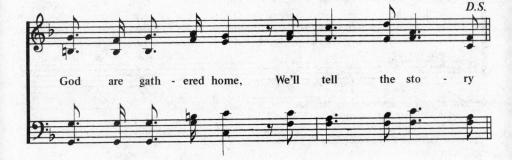

God are gath - ered home, We'll tell the sto - ry

56 Throw Out the Lifeline

E. S. U.

Edward S. Ufford
Arr. by Don Peterman

1. Throw out the life - line a - cross the dark wave!
2. Throw out the life - line with hand quick and strong —
3. Throw out the life - line to dan - ger - fraught men,
4. Soon will the sea - son of res - cue be o'er,

There is a broth - er* whom some - one should save; —
Why do you tar - ry, why lin - ger so long?
Sink - ing in an - guish where you've nev - er been;
Soon will they drift to e - ter - ni - ty's shore;

Some - bod - y's broth - er!** Oh, who then will dare
See! he is sink - ing! Oh, has - ten to - day,
Winds of temp - ta - tion and bil - lows of woe
Haste then, my broth - er,** no time for de - lay,

* "Sinner" may be substituted for "brother."
** "Neighbor" may be substituted for "brother."

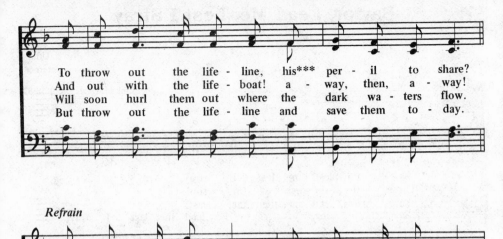

To throw out the life - line, his*** per - il to share?
And out with the life - boat! a - way, then, a - way!
Will soon hurl them out where the dark wa - ters flow.
But throw out the life - line and save them to - day.

Refrain

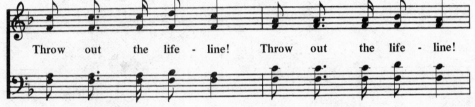

Throw out the life - line! Throw out the life - line!

Some - one is drift - ing a - way; Throw out the life - line!

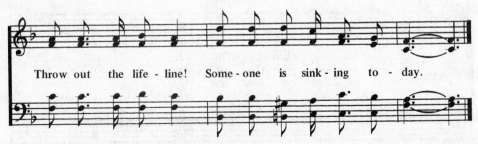

Throw out the life - line! Some - one is sink - ing to - day.

*** "All" may be substituted for "his."

Savior, Lead Me, Lest I Stray

F. M. D.

Frank M. Davis, 1839-1896

1. Sav - ior, lead me, lest I stray,
2. Thou the ref - uge of my soul,
3. Sav ior, lead me, then at last,
1. Sav - ior, lead me, lest I stray,

Gen - tly lead me all the way;
When life's storm - y bil - lows roll,
When the storm of life is past,
Gen - tly lead me all the way;

I am safe when by Thy side,
I am safe when Thou art nigh,
To the land of end - less day,
I am safe when by Thy side,

I would in Thy love a - bide.
All my hopes on Thee re - ly.
Where all tears are wiped a - way.
I would in Thy love a - bide.

Refrain

Lead me, lead me, Sav - ior, lead me, lest I
Sav - ior,

stray; Gen - tly down the stream of time,
stray, lest I stray; Gen-tly stream of time,

Lead me, Sav - ior, all the way.
way, all the way.

58   The Storm is Passing Over

Charles Albert Tindley, 1851-1933
Arr. by F. A. Clark

C.A.T.

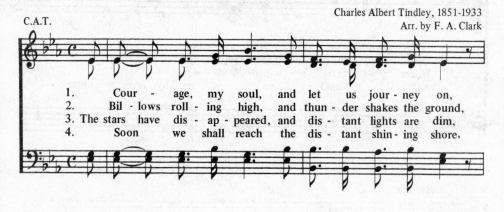

1. Cour - age, my soul, and let us jour - ney on,
2. Bil - lows roll - ing high, and thun - der shakes the ground,
3. The stars have dis - ap - peared, and dis - tant lights are dim,
4. Soon we shall reach the dis - tant shin - ing shore,

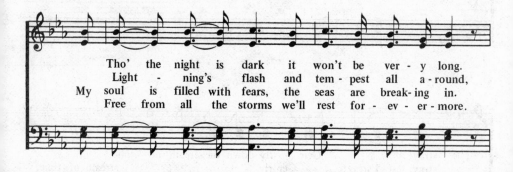

Tho' the night is dark it won't be ver - y long.
Light - ning's flash and tem - pest all a - round,
My soul is filled with fears, the seas are break- ing in.
Free from all the storms we'll rest for - ev - er - more.

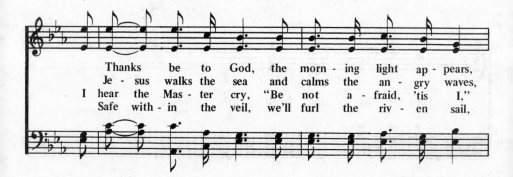

Thanks be to God, the morn - ing light ap - pears,
Je - sus walks the sea and calms the an - gry waves,
I hear the Mas - ter cry, "Be not a - fraid, 'tis I,"
Safe with - in the veil, we'll furl the riv - en sail,

And the storm is pass - ing o - ver, Hal - le - lu - jah!
And the storm is pass - ing o - ver, Hal - le - lu - jah!
And the storm will soon be o - ver, Hal - le - lu - jah!
And the storms will all be o - ver, Hal - le - lu - jah!

Refrain

Hal - le - lu - jah! Hal - le - lu - jah!

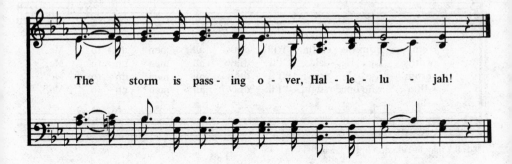

The storm is pass - ing o - ver, Hal - le - lu - jah!

59 Lift Him Up

Johnson Oatman, Jr., alt.

B. B. Beall

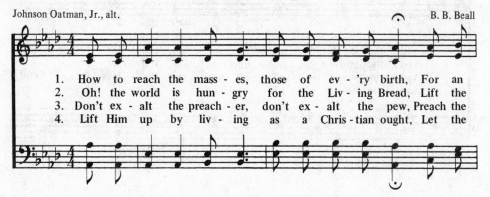

1. How to reach the mass - es, those of ev - 'ry birth, For an
2. Oh! the world is hun - gry for the Liv - ing Bread, Lift the
3. Don't ex - alt the preach - er, don't ex - alt the pew, Preach the
4. Lift Him up by liv - ing as a Chris - tian ought, Let the

an - swer Je - sus gave the key; "And I, if I be lift - ed
Sav - ior up for them to see; Trust Him and do not doubt the
gos - pel sim - ple, full and free; Prove Him and you will find that
world in you the Sav - ior see; Then all will glad - ly fol - low

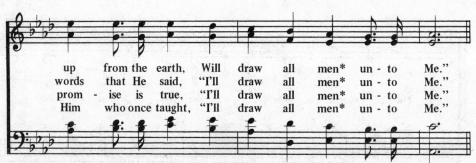

up   from the earth, Will draw all men* un - to Me."
words   that He said, "I'll draw all men* un - to Me."
prom - ise is true, "I'll draw all men* un - to Me."
Him   who once taught, "I'll draw all men* un - to Me."

* "folk" may be substituted for "men."

Refrain

Lift Him up, Lift Him up,
Lift the pre - cious Sav - ior up, Lift the pre - cious Sav - ior up,

Still He speaks from e - ter - ni - ty: "And I, if I be lift - ed

up from the earth, Will draw all men* un - to Me."

*"folk" may be substituted for "men."

60   I Have Found at Last the Savior

Charles Albert Tindley, 1851-1933
C. A. T.
Arr. by F. A. Clark

1. I have found at last the Sav - ior, Of whom I've of - ten
2. I have prom - ised I would fol - low, How - ev - er rough the
3. Christ is now my sum of plea - sure, Count-ing all things else but
4. Should the world in arms con - front me, Though the host of hell com -
5. By and by when war is o - ver, And the saints are gath - 'ring

heard, And I have the pre - cious fa - vor, He has
way, Leav - ing all things of to - mor - row, I will
dross, I have found my rich - est trea - sure, A -
bine, In His name I'll win the vic - t'ry, His
home, In the pres - ence of Je - ho - vah, Where the

prom - ised in His word: O the joy that comes to
trust Him just to - day: For the morn - ing doth ap -
round the sa - cred Cross: My soul is sat - is -
word the con - queror's sign. Our Lord for - ev - er
pil - grim ne'er shall roam: My Je - sus will be

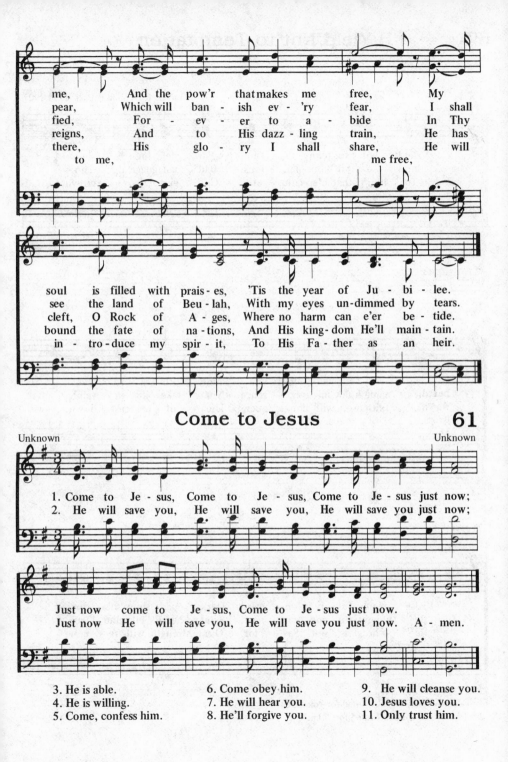

me, And the pow'r that makes me free, My
pear, Which will ban - ish ev - 'ry fear, I shall
fied, For - ev - er to a - bide In Thy
reigns, And to His dazz - ling train, He has
there, His glo - ry I shall share, He will

to me, me free,

soul is filled with prais - es, 'Tis the year of Ju - bi - lee.
see the land of Beu - lah, With my eyes un-dimmed by tears.
cleft, O Rock of A - ges, Where no harm can e'er be - tide.
bound the fate of na - tions, And His king-dom He'll main - tain.
in - tro - duce my spir - it, To His Fa - ther as an heir.

Come to Jesus 61

Unknown   Unknown

1. Come to Je - sus, Come to Je - sus, Come to Je - sus just now;
2. He will save you, He will save you, He will save you just now;

Just now come to Je - sus, Come to Je - sus just now.
Just now He will save you, He will save you just now. A - men.

3. He is able.   6. Come obey him.   9. He will cleanse you.
4. He is willing.   7. He will hear you.   10. Jesus loves you.
5. Come, confess him.   8. He'll forgive you.   11. Only trust him.

62   Yield Not to Temptation

H. R. P.   Horatio Richmond Palmer, 1834-1907

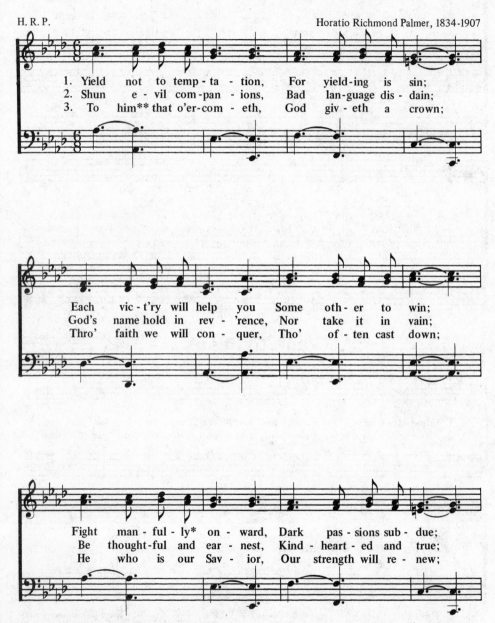

1. Yield not to temp-ta - tion, For yield-ing is sin;
2. Shun e - vil com-pan - ions, Bad lan-guage dis - dain;
3. To him** that o'er-com - eth, God giv - eth a crown;

Each vic - t'ry will help you Some oth - er to win;
God's name hold in rev - 'rence, Nor take it in vain;
Thro' faith we will con - quer, Tho' of - ten cast down;

Fight man - ful - ly* on - ward, Dark pas - sions sub - due;
Be thought-ful and ear - nest, Kind - heart - ed and true;
He who is our Sav - ior, Our strength will re - new;

* "valiantly" may be substituted for "manfully."
** "those" may be substituted for "him."

Look ev - er to Je - sus, He'll car - ry you through.
Look ev - er to Je - sus, He'll car - ry you through.
Look ev - er to Je - sus, He'll car - ry you through.

Refrain

Ask the Sav-ior to help you, Com - fort, strength-en,and keep you;

He is will-ing to aid you, He will car - ry you through.

63 What Are They Doing in Heaven?

C. A. T.

Charles Albert Tindley, 1851-1933

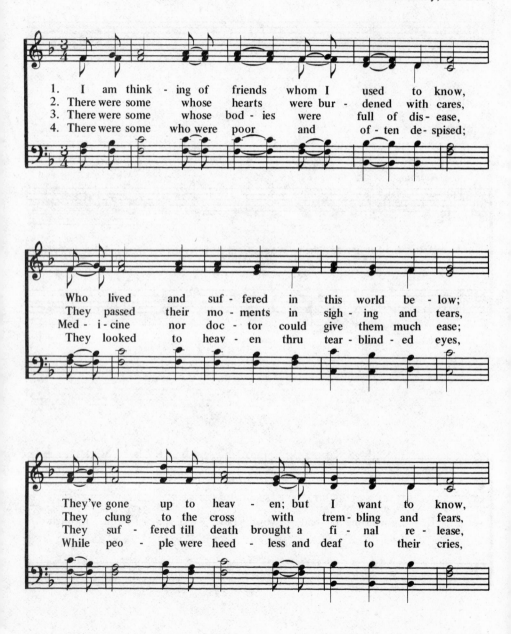

1. I am think - ing of friends whom I used to know,
2. There were some whose hearts were bur - dened with cares,
3. There were some whose bod - ies were full of dis - ease,
4. There were some who were poor and of - ten de- spised;

Who lived and suf - fered in this world be - low;
They passed their mo - ments in sigh - ing and tears,
Med - i - cine nor doc - tor could give them much ease;
They looked to heav - en thru tear - blind - ed eyes,

They've gone up to heav - en; but I want to know,
They clung to the cross with trem - bling and fears,
They suf - fered till death brought a fi - nal re - lease,
While peo - ple were heed - less and deaf to their cries,

What they are do - ing now.
But what are they do - ing now?
But what are they do - ing now?
But what are they do - ing now?

Refrain

What are they do - ing in heav - en to - day? Where sin and

sor - row are all done a - way, And peace a - bounds like a

riv - er, they say; Oh, what are they do - ing there now?

64 Thy Way, O Lord

Nina B. Jackson

E. C. Deas

1. Thy way, O Lord, not mine, Thy will be done, not mine;
2. Thy way, O Lord, not mine, Let glo - ry all be Thine;
3. Hide me from self, O Lord, May I at - tend Thy word;
4. Sub - mis - sive - ly, I bow; With strength and grace en - dow

Since Thou for me didst bleed, And now doth in - ter - cede,
Keep me, lest I may stray, Near Thee from day to day;
Send pride be - yond re - call, Let each as - sail - er fall,
This wea - ry, sin - ful heart; Shield from each cru - el dart;

Each day I sim - ply plead, Thy will be done.
Teach me to watch and pray, Thy will be done.
Be Thou my all in all, Thy will be done.
May I from Thee ne'er part, Thy will be done.

Refrain

Thy will, Thy will be done, Thy will, Thy will be done;
Thy will be done, Thy will be done;

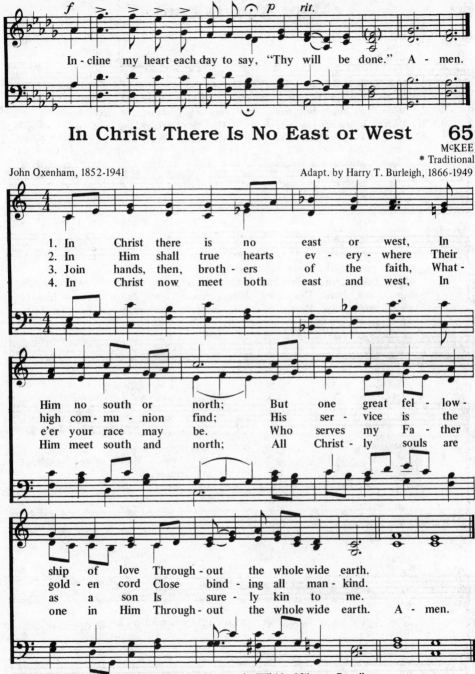

In-cline my heart each day to say, "Thy will be done." A - men.

In Christ There Is No East or West 65

MᶜKEE
* Traditional

John Oxenham, 1852-1941

Adapt. by Harry T. Burleigh, 1866-1949

1. In Christ there is no east or west, In
2. In Him shall true hearts ev - ery - where Their
3. Join hands, then, broth - ers of the faith, What -
4. In Christ now meet both east and west, In

Him no south or north; But one great fel - low -
high com - mu - nion find; His ser - vice is the
e'er your race may be. Who serves my Fa - ther
Him meet south and north; All Christ - ly souls are

ship of love Through - out the whole wide earth.
gold - en cord Close bind - ing all man - kind.
as a son Is sure - ly kin to me.
one in Him Through - out the whole wide earth. A - men.

* This tune came from a Negro Spiritual, "I Went to the Hillside, I Went to Pray."
Words by kind permisssion of Desmond Dunkerly.

66 More About Jesus

Eliza E. Hewitt, 1851-1920

John R. Sweney, 1837-1899

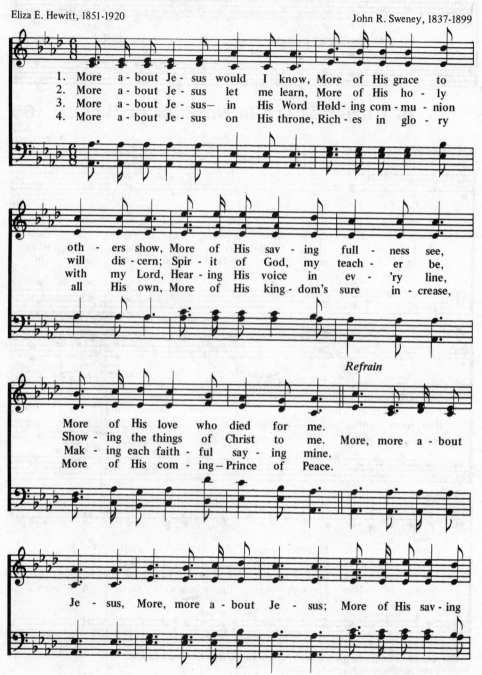

1. More a-bout Je-sus would I know, More of His grace to
2. More a-bout Je-sus let me learn, More of His ho-ly
3. More a-bout Je-sus— in His Word Hold-ing com-mu-nion
4. More a-bout Je-sus on His throne, Rich-es in glo-ry

oth - ers show, More of His sav - ing full - ness see,
will dis - cern; Spir - it of God, my teach - er be,
with my Lord, Hear - ing His voice in ev - 'ry line,
all His own, More of His king - dom's sure in - crease,

Refrain

More of His love who died for me.
Show - ing the things of Christ to me. More, more a - bout
Mak - ing each faith - ful say - ing mine.
More of His com - ing— Prince of Peace.

Je - sus, More, more a - bout Je - sus; More of His sav - ing

full - ness see, More of His love who died for me.

I Surrender All 67

SURRENDER

Judson W. Van De Venter, 1855- 1939

Winfield S. Weeden, 1847-1908

1. All to Je - sus I sur-ren-der, All to Him I free-ly give;
I will ev - er love and trust Him, In His pres-ence dai - ly live.

2. All to Je - sus I sur-ren - der, Hum-bly at His feet I bow;
World - ly plea-sures all for-sak - en, Take me, Je - sus, take me now.

3. All to Je - sus I sur-ren - der, Make me, Sav - ior, whol-ly Thine;
Let me feel the Ho - ly Spir - it, Tru - ly know that Thou art mine.

4. All to Je - sus I sur -ren-der, Lord, I give my-self to Thee;
Fill me with Thy love and pow- er, Let Thy bless-ings fall on me.

Refrain

I sur-ren-der all, I sur-ren-der all,

I sur-ren -der all, I sur-ren-der all,

All to Thee, my bless - ed Sav - ior, I sur-ren - der all.

68   Life's Railway to Heaven

Charles Davis Tillman, 1861-1943
Arr. by J. Jefferson Cleveland, 1937-
and Verolga Nix, 1933-

M. E. Abbey

1. Life is like a moun-tain rail - road, With an   en - gi - neer that's brave;
2. You will roll up grades of   tri - al, You will   cross   the bridge of   strife;
3. You will of -ten find   ob- struc - tions, Look for storms of wind and   rain;
4. As you roll a-cross the tres - tle, Span-ning Jor - dan's swell- ing   tide;

We must   make the run suc-cess-ful From the   cra - dle   to the grave;
See that Christ is your con-duc-tor On this   light-ning train of   life;
On   a   fill   or curve or tres - tle, They will   al - most ditch your train;
You be - hold the Un - ion De- pot In - to which your train will glide;

Watch the   curves, the fills,   the tun - nels, Nev- er   fal - ter, nev- er quail;
Al - ways mind -ful of   ob- struc - tion, Do your   du - ty, nev- er fail;
Put   your trust a- lone in   Je - sus; Nev- er   fal - ter, nev- er fail;
There you'll meet the Su - p'rin-tend - ent, God the Fa -ther, God the Son,

Keep your hand up-on the throt-tle, And your eye up-on the rail.
Keep your hand up-on the throt-tle, And your eye up-on the rail.
Keep your hand up-on the throt-tle, And your eye up-on the rail.
With a heart-y, joy-ous plau-dit, "Wea-ry pil-grim, wel-come home."

Refrain

Bless-ed Sav-ior, Thou wilt guide us, Till we reach that bliss-ful shore,

Where the an-gels wait to join us In Thy praise for-ev-er-more.

69 My Heavenly Father Watches Over Me

Charles H. Gabriel, 1856-1932
Arr. by J. Jefferson Cleveland, 1937-
and Verolga Nix, 1933-

W.C. Martin

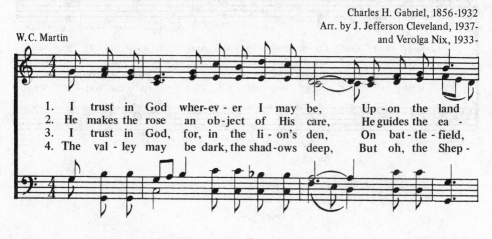

1. I trust in God wher-ev - er I may be, Up - on the land
2. He makes the rose an ob-ject of His care, He guides the ea -
3. I trust in God, for, in the li - on's den, On bat - tle - field,
4. The val - ley may be dark, the shad-ows deep, But oh, the Shep-

or on the roll - ing sea, For come what may,
gle thru the path - less air, And sure - ly He
or in the pris - on pen, Thru praise or blame,
herd guards His lone - ly sheep, And thru the gloom,

From day to day,
Re - mem - bers me, My heav'n-ly Fa - ther watch-es o - ver
Thru flood or flame,
He'll lead me home,

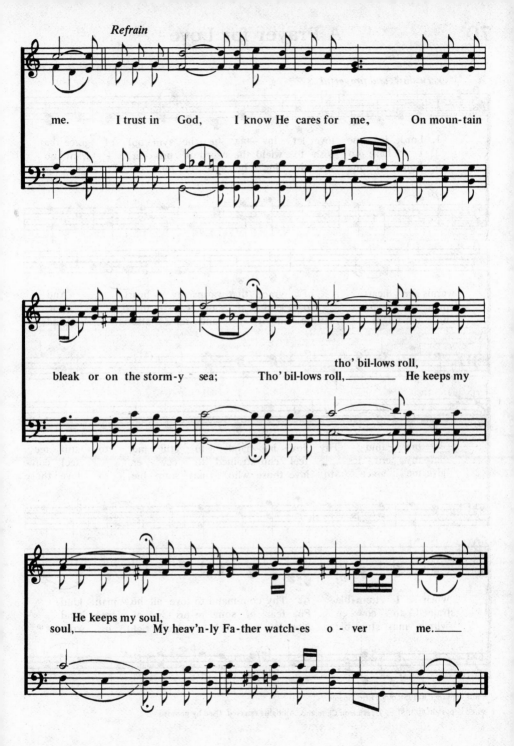

Refrain

me. I trust in God, I know He cares for me, On moun-tain bleak or on the storm-y sea; Tho' bil-lows roll,_____ tho' bil-lows roll, He keeps my soul, He keeps my soul,_____ My heav'n-ly Fa-ther watch-es o - ver me._____

70 A Prayer for Love

C. Eric Lincoln, 1924-

J. Jefferson Cleveland, 1937-

Very slow and prayerful

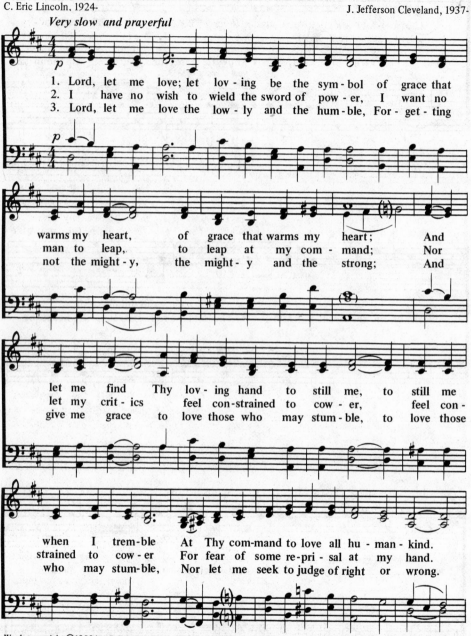

1. Lord, let me love; let lov - ing be the sym - bol of grace that warms my heart, of grace that warms my heart; And let me find Thy lov - ing hand to still me, to still me when I trem - ble At Thy com-mand to love all hu - man - kind.

2. I have no wish to wield the sword of pow - er, I want no man to leap, to leap at my com - mand; Nor let my crit - ics feel con-strained to cow - er, feel con-strained to cow - er For fear of some re-pri - sal at my hand.

3. Lord, let me love the low - ly and the hum - ble, For - get - ting not the might - y, the might - y and the strong; And give me grace to love those who may stum - ble, to love those who may stum - ble, Nor let me seek to judge of right or wrong.

Lord, let me love, though love may be the los-ing Of ev-'ry
Lord, teach me mer - cy; let me be the win - ner Of ev-'ry
Lord, let my par - ish be the world un - bound-ed, Let love of

earth-ly trea-sure I pos - sess. Lord, make Thy love the pat-tern
man's re - spect and sim - ple love. For I have known Thy mer-cy,
race and clan be at an end. Let ev -'ry hate-ful doc-trine

of my choos-ing. And let Thy will dic-tate my hap-pi-
though a sin - ner. When - ev - er I have sought Thy peace a-
be con-found-ed That in - ter-dicts the love of friend for

D.C.   Optional ending

ness._____   A - men.   A-men.   A - men.   A - men.
bove._____
friend._____

71   Love Lifted Me

James Rowe, 1865-1933

Howard E. Smith, 1863-1918

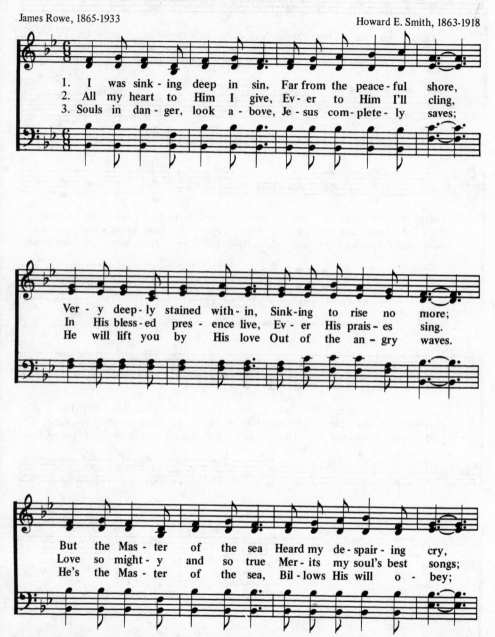

1. I was sink-ing deep in sin, Far from the peace-ful shore,
2. All my heart to Him I give, Ev-er to Him I'll cling,
3. Souls in dan-ger, look a-bove, Je-sus com-plete-ly saves;

Ver-y deep-ly stained with-in, Sink-ing to rise no more;
In His bless-ed pres-ence live, Ev-er His prais-es sing.
He will lift you by His love Out of the an-gry waves.

But the Mas-ter of the sea Heard my de-spair-ing cry,
Love so might-y and so true Mer-its my soul's best songs;
He's the Mas-ter of the sea, Bil-lows His will o-bey;

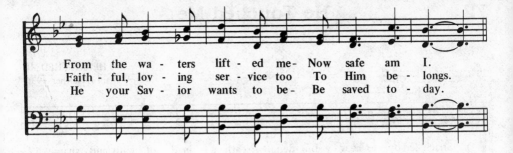

From the wa - ters lift - ed me— Now safe am I.
Faith - ful, lov - ing ser - vice too To Him be - longs.
He your Sav - ior wants to be— Be saved to - day.

Refrain

Love lift - ed me, Love lift - ed me, When noth - ing
e - ven me, e - ven me,

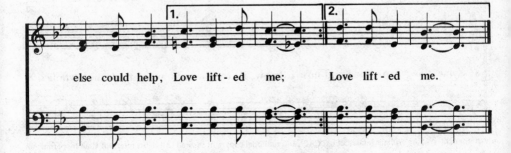

1.
else could help, Love lift - ed me;
2.
Love lift - ed me.

72 He Touched Me

W. J. G.

HE TOUCHED ME
William J. Gaither, 1936-

1. Shack-led by a heav-y bur-den, 'Neath a load of guilt and shame,
2. Since I met this bless-ed Sav-ior, Since He cleansed and made me whole,

Then the hand of Je-sus touched me, And now I am no long-er the same.
I will nev-er cease to praise Him, I'll shout it while e-ter-ni-ty rolls.

Refrain

He touched me, O He touched me, And O the joy that floods my soul;

Some-thing hap-pened, and now I know, He touched me and made me whole.

A Historical
Account of the
Negro Spiritual

Spirituals emanated from the heart of the ante-bellum Negro slave as forceful outflowings of religious passion. It is not known exactly when these powerful songs began to spring forth; however, history confirms the use of these songs as *the music* of the pre–Civil War "invisible church."[1] Wyatt Tee Walker states that "the Spiritual music form . . . developed as an integral part of worship in these 'invisible churches'. In the preliterate era of slavery, the fuel of the 'invisible church' was the musical expression constantly fed by the oral tradition" (19:31-32).[2] E. Franklin Frazier puts it this way: "From the beginning of religious expression among the slaves, . . . preaching on the part of the leader was important. This preaching consisted of singing sacred songs which have come to be known as the Spirituals" (11:25).

These songs—variously called Negro spirituals, jubilees, folk songs, shout songs, sorrow songs, slave songs, slave melodies, minstrel songs, and religious songs—are most commonly known as Negro spirituals because of the deep religious feeling they express. Many of these spirituals were influenced by the surrounding conditions in which the slaves lived. These conditions were negative and degrading, to say the least; yet, miraculously, a body of approximately six thousand independent spirituals exists today—melodies that were, for the most part, handed down from generation to generation. The spirituals, which speak of life and death, suffering and sorrow, love and judgment, grace and hope, justice and mercy, were born out of this tradition. They are the songs of a people weary at heart. The Negro spirituals are the songs of an unhappy people, and yet they are the most beautiful expression of human experience born this side of the seas. One noted musicologist has suggested that Beethoven would have delighted in Negro spirituals. Brahms, he thinks, would have borrowed them as Dvorak did.

The music is more ancient than the words. The Africans celebrated all important events such as marriages, births, and deaths with music. Even work, play, and public humor were accompanied by music. Although rhythm was important to the music, the words were primary because they were derived from the particular event. The

---

1. "Invisible churches" were secret places where the Negro slaves held worship services. They met from place to place on individual plantations, sometimes on nearby plantations, and even in the forest bush.
2. Numbers in parentheses refer to entries in the numbered bibliography at the end of "A Historical Account of the Negro Spiritual."

content and mood of the occasion often dictated the use of specific instruments and hand clapping.

The Negro spirituals, as originated in America, tell of exile and trouble, of strife and hiding; they grope toward some unseen power and sigh for rest in the end. "But through all the sorrow of the sorrow songs," as William E. B. DuBois points out, "there breathes a hope—a faith in the ultimate justice of things" (5:253).

A close look at the musical *form* and characteristics of the Negro spiritual reveals that *rhythm* is its primary characteristic. It is here that the spiritual shows one of the greatest signs of originality. Intricacy of rhythms has added to the difficulty facing the folklorist in notating these songs as they were passed on from generation to generation. The majority of spirituals are written in quadruple meter ($\frac{4}{4}$); yet many of these have a feel of duple meter ($\frac{2}{4}$). Spirituals written in triple meter ($\frac{3}{4}$) are rarities. The special feature of rhythm known as syncopation is very common to the spiritual and often causes the original meter to be changed within the course of the composition.

From the standpoint of *melodic variety,* spirituals are usually classified in three groups: the "call and response" chant, which involves a leader (soloist) and a group (choir or congregation) that responds to a short melodic statement by the leader (e.g., "There's a Great Camp Meeting" and "Great Day"); the syncopated, segmented melody in which the musical line is often made up of short segments or short rhythmic patterns (often repeated) with a syncopated figure, instead of a complete, sustained phrase. The tempo is usually fast, and bodily movement is stimulated by a rhythmic swing (e.g., "Ain't Dat Good News" and "Ev'ry Time I Feel the Spirit"). The third group is the slow, sustained, long-phrase melody in which the tempo is slow and the phrase line long and sustained (e.g., "Deep River" and "My Lord! What a Mourning"). Spiritual melodies, while vocally diatonic and highly ornamented, are often plaintive, often nostalgic, yet dignified, beautiful, and appealing.

The *scales* used by the Negro in the spirituals were, for the most part, the conventional major and minor, the pentatonic, and mixed or modal scales. He either consciously or unconsciously avoided the fourth and seventh degrees of the major scale, with the pentatonic scale being the automatic result. Examples of spirituals utilizing this scale are "Steal Away" and "Nobody Knows the Trouble I See." Very distinct mixed scales were developed (and frequently utilized) by using notes that were foreign to the conventional major and minor scales. The most widely used of these are the "flatted third"[3] (e.g., "Oh! What a Beautiful City" and "No Hidin' Place") and the "flatted seventh" (e.g., "Roll, Jordan, Roll" and "There's a Great Camp Meeting"). The "flatted sixth" is sometimes used, and frequently more than one altered tone is found in the same song. Also, altered tones and their normal counterparts are frequently contained in the same song. The minor scale and the medieval ecclesiastical modes are used only to a small degree; consequently, there is

---

3. The flatted third is the feature note of the blues.

a small number of spirituals based on these compositional techniques. Some songs defy scalar classification because of extremely vague melodic implications.

Clearly defined *keys* and *chords* appear in many spirituals, while in others keys and chords are difficult to outline and confirm. While key or tonal centers for the most part, remain stable, they are sometimes changed without preparation. Most spirituals show the strict use of the common chords, I, IV, and V, which serve to weave fabrics of consonances. Dissonances are very sparingly used, and when they are, they serve a specific purpose and certainly do not disturb the overall harmonic fabric.

Musical *texture* refers to the horizontal and vertical elements of music. Horizontal elements are the successive sounds forming melodies, while vertical elements are those simultaneous sounds forming harmonies. We generally refer to music as having a *monophonic* texture when there is a single melodic line without additional parts or accompaniment; a *polyphonic* texture when two or more simultaneous melodies of individual design are combined; or a *homophonic* texture when a single melody is supported by an accompaniment in chordal style. Initially, most of the Negro spirituals were monophonic in texture; however, some were homophonic and some heterophonic.[4]

The chief vehicle for the *performance* of the Negro spiritual was the human voice.[5] The vocal performance of the Negro spiritual was, without a doubt, unique, for it was this feat that provided the spiritual with its contour, rhythm, texture, melody, tempo, and text. The listener's response to and the effectiveness of the spiritual was determined, in large part, by its performance. Accompanying the singing of the spiritual at all times was some form of body movement—shouting, dancing, hand clapping, foot tapping, foot stamping, or swaying of the body. The singers were bound by no rules; yet, chants, hums, wailings, shouts, glides, turns, groans, moans, word interjections, and so on were not used indiscriminately, as might appear, but were used as special devices to urge the singer on to exciting and climactic performances. These practices are typically African. Also, the art and the importance of musical *improvisation* in the African tradition were bequeathed to the originators of the Negro spiritual; therefore, improvisation became one of the main stylistic features of this folk song. Even the words were often improvised to correspond with a certain event or situation.

The *texts* or *words* of the spirituals generally represented the feeling of the songs; however, not always. Howard Thurman suggests that the majority of the texts came from the Old and New Testaments of the Holy Bible; yet, the world of nature and the common personal experiences of religion also provided texts (18:18-33).

The Old Testament is much more extensively represented in spiritual texts, for through its stories of the Hebrews in bondage, it immediately spoke to the slaves. Hence, "Go Down, Moses" and "Didn't My Lord Deliver Daniel?"

---

4. Heterophony is the simultaneous use of slightly ornamented versions of the same melody by two or more performers.
5. Many regard the *performance* of vocal music the single most vital factor in slave music.

The New Testament records the life and death of Jesus, and though some spiritual texts are drawn from it, very few depict the nativity of Jesus. His death and suffering were more personal to the slaves than his birth, hence "Were You There When They Crucified My Lord?" and "He Nevuh Said a Mumbalin' Word." Nevertheless, there are a few Christmas spirituals that depict the miraculous birth. "Go, Tell It on the Mountain" and "De Glory Manger" are examples.

The world of nature furnished the slaves with ideas that were easily transformed into religious truth. The spirituals "Deep River" and "Roll, Jordan, Roll" contain developments drawn from nature. The Promised Land, Heaven, and "over Jordan" were thought of as actual places (on this or the otherside of terra firma) where they (the slaves) could and would go someday to be rid of trials and tribulations.

The religious experience of the slaves was rich and full, consequently their inner emotional expressions and aspirations burst forth in many spirituals that outlined varying aspects of their desires. Freedom from slavery and freedom from life itself were often synonymous in thought, as is depicted in the spiritual "Oh, Freedom." Release in death sometimes became the ultimate hope and goal, as is expressed in "Steal Away" and in "Swing Low, Sweet Chariot."

Hildred Roach informs us that "despite the overabundance of Biblical words used in the majority of spirituals, their functions were not purely religious. They were constantly used in the search of freedom, in religious services, to teach, gossip, scold, signal, or to delight in the telling of tales. . . . They also relieved the minds and bodies of the enslaved and they served more significantly as a practical means of informing the slaves of their own affairs, i.e., social politics, deliverance, escape, or satire" (15:26). The texts of many spirituals, then, are highly specialized. An *eternality of message* is depicted in "God Is a God":

> God is a God
> God don't never change!
> God is a God
> An' He always will be God!

Dual, or *coded meaning* appears in "There's a Great Camp Meeting":

> Walk together children
> Don't you get weary,
> There's a great camp meeting in the promised land.

Others in this category are "Steal Away" and "O Mary, Don't You Weep, Don't You Mourn." Numerous spirituals are filled with amazing images. The "word painting" found in "Hush, Hush, Somebody's Callin' Mah Name," "Keep A-Inchin' Along," and "Somebody's Knocking at Your Door" is superb.

Many of the spirituals might have served as religious songs with political significance because of the nature of their texts. Such spirituals are: "De Gospel Train" ("Git on Board, Little Children"), "Steal Away," "Didn't My Lord Deliver Daniel?" "Deep River," and "Roll, Jordan, Roll."

These early spirituals were not just songs, as can be clearly discerned in the foregoing discourse. Not only were they unceasing variations on a theme, but they were, as well, Negro religious (and social) songs sung by a group of people whose minds and hearts were bent on expressions of feelings, with minuscule regard for sound effect, vocal beauty, or proper harmonic progression.

The development of the spiritual continued beyond the act of emancipation of the slaves. In the 1870s, with the Fisk Jubilee Singers of Fisk University (Nashville, Tennessee), the early spiritual went through an artistic metamorphosis that not only changed its form and appearance but also helped to make it a permanent American musical art form. With George L. White[6] and the Jubilee Singers, the spiritual, as performed in the "invisible church," praise house, and cotton fields, became an artistic, "concertized" choral form which not only the United States but the entire world enjoyed through tours by these fantastic singers and performers. The success of the Jubilee Singers prompted other Black institutions to establish similar groups. The Hampton Institute Singers became extremely popular under the guidance of R. Nathaniel Dett and, along with all the other groups, helped establish a tradition of spiritual singing that has been maintained to the present day and can be heard in universities, colleges, high schools, and in Black churches throughout the nation. Wyatt Tee Walker justifiably states that "a great debt is owed to the Fisk Jubilee Singers and the other Black university choirs of that era who kept alive the original Black sacred music of the painful past" (19:62).

By the last decade of the nineteenth century, many talented Black composers had studied or were studying either privately with the nation's most renowned teachers or at the nation's leading music schools and conservatories, including Oberlin, the New England Conservatory, the American Conservatory (Chicago), and the National Conservatory (New York). Almost all of these composers consciously utilized the folk music of their people as a source of inspiration for their composed music, thereby preserving the Black spiritual tradition in various Western forms. In 1914, R. Nathaniel Dett produced the first of numerous "anthemized" spirituals, "Listen to the Lambs," and other composers followed suit. Harry T. Burleigh was the first to arrange and perform spirituals in the style of the European art song for solo voice. His 1916 arrangement and performance of "Deep River" became a model for other composers and performers. Eileen Southern states, "After Burleigh, many concert singers developed the tradition of closing their recitals with a group of Negro Spirituals" (17:287). Included in this illustrious number were (or are) Marian Anderson, Paul Robeson, Dorothy Manor, Roland Hayes, Camilla Williams, Todd Duncan, Mattiwilda Dobbs, Robert McFerrin, Adele Addison, Betty Allen, Leontyne Price, Shirley Verrett, George Shirley, Martina Arroyo, and Simon Estes.

Other Black composers wrote vocal and instrumental arrangements of spirituals but, in addition, utilized them as thematic material for vocal and instrumental compositions. This group includes Edward Boatner, Clarence Cameron White,

---

6. George L. White was the young, White music instructor at Fisk who organized, trained, and named the original Fisk Jubilee Singers.

Willis Lawrence James, Hall Johnson, William L. Dawson, John W. Work, Sr., Frederick Hall, R. Nathaniel Dett, Eva Jessye, James Weldon and J. Rosamond Johnson, Samuel Coleridge-Taylor, William Grant Still, and, more recently, Florence Price, Margaret Bonds, Undine Smith Moore, and Lena Johnson McLin.

White symphonic composers were also fascinated with the spiritual around the turn of the century and produced several symphonies and other instrumental works based on themes utilizing the spiritual idiom. Perhaps the most notable were the Czechoslovakian composer Anton Dvorak (greatly influenced by his student, Harry T. Burleigh) and the American composer George Gershwin.

The influence and development of the spiritual has indeed been far-reaching. Because of their messages and emotions, spirituals became the penetrating force in both popular and classical music of the contemporary era. Despite the fact that great debate has been engaged in concerning the influence of the spiritual, it cannot be denied—and scholars have concurred—that minstrel songs, jazz, blues, country music, popular songs, ring-game songs, swing, White rock, "soul" music, and gospel music are directly related in origin to the spiritual.

Many of the early gospel songs were simply arrangements and adaptations of spirituals.[7] Among the adapters were Thomas A. Dorsey, Sallie Martin, Roberta Martin, Robert Johnson, Myrtle Jackson, Kenneth Morris, and James Cleveland.

Out of the reservoir of Negro spirituals were created the freedom songs of the nonviolent movement in the South during the peak of the demonstrations for social justice and human dignity. It is difficult for anyone to deny that the spiritual is the foundation of Black music in this country and, oh, what a solid foundation it is!

In conclusion, these songs of the soul and of the soil have enriched American music and the music of the world. From them have developed the "gospel" hymn of White Protestantism, the syncopated rhythm and jazz of the world of art, and a wealth of materials used by great composers. They are the articulate message of an oppressed people. They are the music of a captive people who used this artful expression to embrace the virtues of Christianity: patience, love, freedom, faith, and hope.

The slaves were not simply singing a song, they were expressing a point of view:

> Go down, Moses, way down in Egypt land,
> Tell ole Pharaoh to let my people go.

That point of view was that the God of justice and the God of Jesus is on the side of the oppressed. That is the heart of the Bible and the fulcrum of liberation.

These spirituals are offered here as songs to be sung wherever people gather to glorify God's name. The promise from Him is, "I will be in their midst."

J. Jefferson Cleveland
in collaboration with William B. McClain

---

7. Lena McLin differentiates between the Negro spiritual and Black gospel thusly: "A Spiritual is a *folk song,* originated by the Black American and handed down from generation to generation, which must have a *personal* relationship with the deity. A Gospel is a *composed song,* but the singer expresses this music in a personal style, free, unrestricted in any way. The singer may add or take away (you can't do that with the Spiritual) but the basic line remains the same" (2:40).

Numbered Bibliography

1. Cone, James H. *The Spirituals and the Blues.* New York: The Seabury Press, 1972.
2. De Lerma, Dominique-René. *Black Music in Our Culture.* Kent, Ohio: Kent State University Press, 1970.
3. Dett, R. Nathaniel. *Religious Folk-Songs of the Negro.* Hampton, Virginia: Hampton Institute Press, 1927.
4. Dixon, Christa K. *Negro Spirituals: From Bible to Folksong.* Philadelphia: Fortress Press, 1976.
5. DuBois, W. E. Burghardt. *The Souls of Black Folk.* New York: Washington Square Press, 1970.
6. Eskew, Harry, and McElrath, Hugh T. *Sing with Understanding.* Nashville: Broadman Press, 1980.
7. Hayes, Roland. *My Songs.* Boston: Little, Brown, 1948.
8. Johnson, James Weldon, and Johnson, J. Rosamond. *The Books of American Negro Spirituals.* New York: Viking Press, a Viking Compass Book, 1969.
9. Jones, Leroi. *Black Music.* New York: William Morrow, 1967.
10. Krehbiel, H. E. *Afro-American Folksongs.* New York: Frederick Ungar, 1962.
11. Lincoln, C. Eric. *The Black Church Since Frazier.* Bound with *The Negro Church in America,* by E. Franklin Frazier. New York: Schocken Books, 1973.
12. Locke, Alain. *The Negro and His Music and Negro Art: Past and Present.* New York: Arno Press, 1969.
13. Lovell, John, Jr. *Black Song: The Forge and the Flame.* New York: Macmillan, 1972.
14. McClain, William B. *The Soul of Black Worship.* Madison, N.J.: Drew University, 1980.
15. Roach, Hildred. *Black American Music: Past and Present.* Boston: Crescendo Publishing Co., 1973.
16. Roberts, John. *Black Music of Two Worlds.* New York: Praeger, 1972.
17. Southern, Eileen. *The Music of Black Americans: A History.* New York: W. W. Norton, 1971.
18. Thurman, Howard. *Deep River* and *The Negro Spiritual Speaks.* Richmond, Ind.: Friends United Press, 1975.
19. Walker, Wyatt Tee. *Somebody's Calling My Name.* Valley Forge, Pa.: The Judson Press, 1979.
20. Work, John W. *American Negro Songs and Spirituals.* New York: Bonanza Books, 1940.

74 My Soul's Been Anchored in de Lord

Traditional

Traditional
Arr. by J. Jefferson Cleveland, 1937-

Lively and rhythmically

In de Lord, in de Lord, My soul's been an-chored in de Lord.

1. Be - fo' I'd stay in hell one day
2. Goin' shout an' pray an' nev - er stop
My soul's been an - chored in de

Lord. I'd sing an' pray my - self a - way.
Un - til I reach de moun-tain-top.
My soul's been an-chored in de

O Lord!___ O Lord!___

Lord, My soul's been an-chored in de Lord, My soul's been an-chored in de Lord.

Go, Tell It on the Mountain 75

Traditional
Adapt. by J. W. W.

Traditional
Arr. by John W. Work, 1901-1967

Refrain Unison

Go, tell it on the moun - tain, O - ver the hills and ev - ery - where,

Fine

Go, tell it on the moun - tain That Je - sus Christ is born.

Harmony

1. While shep - herds kept their watch - ing O'er si - lent flocks by night,
2. The shep - herds feared and trem - bled When lo! a - bove the earth
3. Down in a low - ly man - ger The hum - ble Christ was born,

D.C.

Be - hold through-out the heav - ens There shone a ho - ly light.
Rang out the an - gel cho - rus That hailed our Sav - ior's birth.
And God sent us sal - va - tion That bless - ed Christ-mas morn.

76 Lord, I Want to Be a Christian

Traditional

Traditional
Arr. by Dolores Lane,1933-

1. Lord, I want to be a Chris-tian in my heart, in my heart, Lord, I
2. Lord, I want to be more lov-ing in my heart, in my heart, Lord, I
3. Lord, I want to be more ho-ly in my heart, in my heart, Lord, I
4. Lord, I want to be like Je-sus in my heart, in my heart, Lord, I

In my heart_____

want to be a Chris-tian in my heart_____
want to be more lov-ing in my heart_____
want to be more ho-ly in my heart_____
want to be like Je-sus in my heart_____

heart in my

In my heart_____

D. C.

heart, in my heart, in my heart, Lord, I want to be a Chris-tian in my heart.

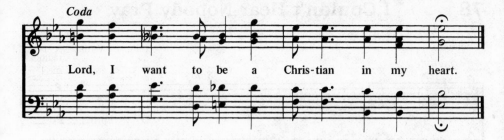

Lord, I want to be a Chris-tian in my heart.

2. Lord, I want to be more loving in my heart, . . .
3. Lord, I want to be more holy in my heart, . . .
4. Lord, I want to be like Jesus in my heart, . . .

Ride On, King Jesus 77

Traditional   Traditional

Majestically
Refrain

Ride on, King Je - sus, No man can a - hin - der me,

Fine

Ride on, King Je-sus, ride on, No man can a - hin-der me.

Verses

1. I was but young when I be-gun, No man can a - hin-der me,

D.C.

But now my race is al - most done,— No man can a - hin-der me.

2. King Jesus rides on a milk-white horse,
   No man can a-hinder me;
   The river of Jordan he did cross,
   No man can a-hinder me.

3. If you want to find your way to God,
   No man can a-hinder me;
   The gospel highway must be trod,
   No man can a-hinder me.

78   I Couldn't Hear Nobody Pray

Traditional

Traditional
Harm. by Verolga Nix, 1933-

79 Rise an' Shine

Traditional

Traditional

Refrain

Oh,— rise an' shine an' give God de glo - ry, glo - ry, Rise an'

shine, an' give God de glo - ry, glo - ry, Rise an' shine, an'

Fine

give God de glo - ry, glo - ry, For de year ob Ju - ber - lee.

Verses

1. Je - sus car - ry de young lambs in his bos - om, bos - om,
Je - sus lead— de ole sheep by still wa - ters, wa - ters,

Car - ry de young lambs in his bos - om, bos - om, Car - ry de
Lead_ de ole sheep by still wa - ters, wa - ters, Lead_ de

young lambs in his bos - om, bos - om, For de year ob Ju - ber - lee.
ole sheep by still wa - ters, wa - ters, For de year ob Ju - ber - lee.

2. Oh, come on, mourners, get you ready, ready,
   Come on, mourners, get you ready, ready,
   Come on, mourners, get you ready, ready,
       For de year ob Juberlee;
   You may keep your lamps trimmed an' burning, burning,
   Keep your lamps trimmed an' burning, burning,
   Keep your lamps trimmed an' burning, burning,
       For de year ob Juberlee.

3. Oh, come on, children, don't be weary, weary,
   Come on, children, don't be weary, weary,
   Come on, children, don't be weary, weary,
       For de year ob Juberlee;
   Oh, don't you hear dem bells a-ringin', ringin',
   Don't you hear dem bells a-ringin', ringin',
   Don't you hear dem bells a-ringin', ringin',
       For de year ob Juberlee?

80 Free at Last

Traditional
Arr. by J. Jefferson Cleveland, 1937-
and Verolga Nix, 1933-

Traditional

Rocking rhythm

Fine

Free at last,___ free at last,___ Thank God a'- might-y I'm free at last.___

Leader

1. Sure - ly been 'buked,   and   sure - ly been scorned,___
2. If   you don't know   that I   been   re - deemed,___

(accomp.)

Response   *Leader*

Thank   God   a'- might - y,   I'm   free   at   last.___   But
                                                                Just

still my soul is - a heav- en born,_____
fol - low me down to Jor - dan's stream,_____

(accomp.)

(Leader)
Oh

D.C. al Fine

Thank God a'- might- y, I'm free at last._____

I'm Gonna Sing

Traditional   Traditional

1. I'm gon - na sing* when the Spir - it says a - Sing, ____ I'm gon - na

sing when the Spir- it says a - Sing, ____ I'm gon - na sing when the

Spir- it says a - Sing, ____ And o - bey the Spir- it of the Lord.____

*2. shout 3. preach 4. pray 5. sing

82   I've Got a Robe

Traditional   Traditional

I've got a robe,* you've got a robe,* All of God's chil-dren got a robe.*

When I get to heav-en goin' to put on my robe,* Go-in' to shout* all o-ver God's

heav-'n. Heav-'n, heav-'n, Ev-'ry-bod-y talk-in' 'bout

heav-'n ain't go-in' there, Heav-'n, heav-'n, ___Goin' to shout* all o-ver God's

*other verses: 2. shoes—walk   5. harp—play
                  3. wings—fly   6. song—sing
                  4. crown—shout   7. prayer—pray

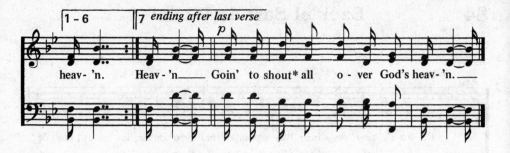

1 – 6 | **7** *ending after last verse*

heav-'n.   Heav-'n____ Goin' to shout* all   o - ver God's heav-'n.____

83

Sometimes I Feel Like a Motherless Chile

Traditional   Traditional

1. Some-times I   feel like a moth-er-less chile,_ Some-times I   feel like a
2. Some-times I   feel like I'm al - mos' gone,_ Some-times I   feel like I'm

moth-er - less   chile,___ Some-times I   feel   like   a   moth-er - less   chile,_
al - mos' gone,_ Some-times I   feel   like   I'm   al - mos'   gone,_

____ A   long   ways   from   home,____ A   long   ways   from home.
____ A   long   ways   from   home,____ A   long   ways   from home.

Then I get down on my knees an'   pray,___ Get down on my knees an' pray.

84 Ezek'el Saw de Wheel

Traditional

Traditional
Harm. by J. Jefferson Cleveland, 1937-

With spirit

E - ze-k'el saw de wheel 'Way up in de mid-dle o' de air, E- ze-k'el saw de

wheel 'Way in de mid-dle o' de air. De big wheel run by faith, De lit- tle wheel run

by de Grace o' God, A wheel in a wheel 'Way in de mid- dle o' de air. *Fine*

Leader ... **Response**

1. Bet - ter min', my sis - ter, how you walk on de cross,
2. Let me tell you, broth- er, what a hypo-crite will do, 'Way in de mid-dle o' de
3. Ol' Sa - tan wears a club - foot shoe,

Yo' foot might slip an' yo' soul be los'.
air, He'll low - rate you an' he'll low-rate me. 'Way in de mid-dle o' de air.
If you don' min', he'll slip it on you.

He's Got the Whole World in His Hands   85

Traditional
Harm. by J. Jefferson Cleveland, 1937--
and Verolga Nix, 1933-

Traditional

Rhythmically

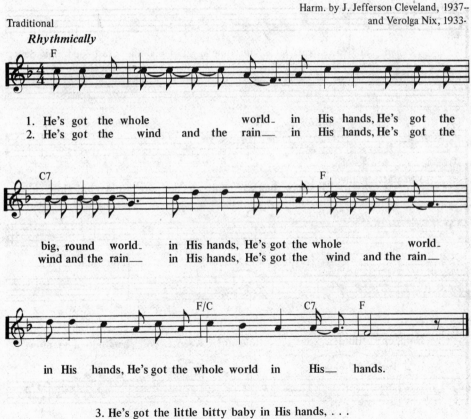

1. He's got the whole world— in His hands, He's got the
2. He's got the wind and the rain— in His hands, He's got the

big, round world— in His hands, He's got the whole world—
wind and the rain— in His hands, He's got the wind and the rain—

in His hands, He's got the whole world in His— hands.

3. He's got the little bitty baby in His hands, . . .
4. He's got you and me, sister, in His hands, . . .
5. He's got you and me, brother, in His hands, . . .

In memory of my mother, Mrs. Geneva C. Cleveland

Hold On

Traditional

Traditional
Arr. by J. Jefferson Cleveland, 1937-

Keep yo' han'___ on de plow, Hold on! Hold on!

No - ra, No - ra, let___ me come in,___ Do's all fast -'ned an' de
No - ra said,___ "Ya lost___ yo' track,___ Can' plow straight an' keep a -

win-ders pinned, Keep yo' han'___ on - a de plow, Hold on! Hold on!
look-in' back," Keep yo' han'___ on - a de plow, Hold on! Hold on!

Hold on!___ Hold on!

Hold on! Hold___ on! Hold on! Keep___ yo' han' on - a de plow,

Calvary

Traditional   Traditional

Very slowly

Cal-va - ry,_____ Cal - va - ry,_ Cal - va - ry,_____ Cal - va - ry,_

Fine

Cal-va - ry,_____ Cal - va - ry,_____ Sure-ly He died on_____ Cal - va - ry._____

Verse (unison)

1. Ev-'ry time I___think a-bout Je-sus, Ev-'ry_ time I ___think a-bout Je-sus,_

D.C.

Ev-'ry time I___think a-bout Je - sus,_ Sure-ly He died on_ Cal - va - ry.

2. Don't you hear the hammer ringing?   4. Don't you hear Him say, "It is finished?"
3. Don't you hear Him calling His Father? 5. Jesus furnished my salvation.
                6. Sinner, do you love my Jesus?

Let Us Break Bread Together

Traditional   Traditional

1. Let us break bread to-geth-er on our knees;＿＿ Let us

break bread to-geth-er on our knees.＿＿ When I fall on my

knees, with my face to the ris-ing sun, Oh,＿ Lord, have mer-cy on me.＿＿

2. Let us drink wine together . . .   3. Let us praise God together . . .

Ole-Time Religion

Traditional

Traditional
Opt. Bass part by
J. Jefferson Cleveland, 1937-

Refrain

Gim-me dat ole-time re - lig - ion, Gim-me dat ole-time re - lig - ion,

Optional Basses

Ole - time re - lig - ion, Gim - me dat ole - time re - lig - ion,

Fine

Gim - me dat ole - time re - lig - ion, It's good e - nough for me.

Gim - me dat ole - time re - lig - ion, It's good e - nough for me.

Verses

1. It was good for my ole fa - ther, It was good for my ole

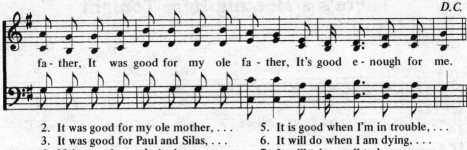

fa - ther, It was good for my ole fa - ther, It's good e - nough for me.

2. It was good for my ole mother, . . .
3. It was good for Paul and Silas, . . .
4. Makes me love ev'rybody, . . .

5. It is good when I'm in trouble, . . .
6. It will do when I am dying, . . .
7. It will take us all to heaven, . . .

His Name So Sweet   90

Traditional
Arr. for male voices
by J. Jefferson Cleveland, 1937-
and Verolga Nix, 1933-

Traditional
Joyfully *Refrain*

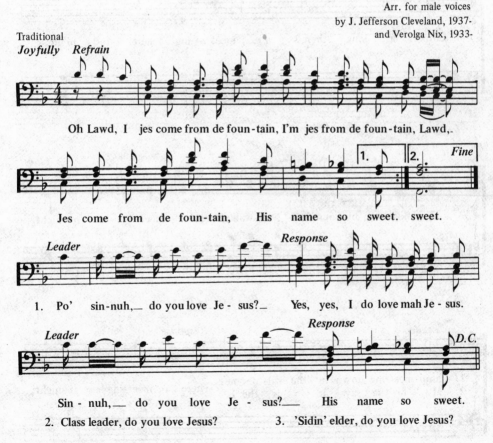

Oh Lawd, I jes come from de foun-tain, I'm jes from de foun-tain, Lawd,

Jes come from de foun-tain, His name so sweet. sweet.

Leader *Response*

1. Po' sin-nuh,— do you love Je - sus?— Yes, yes, I do love mah Je - sus.

Leader *Response*

Sin - nuh,— do you love Je - sus?— His name so sweet.

2. Class leader, do you love Jesus?   3. 'Sidin' elder, do you love Jesus?

91 There's a Meeting Here Tonight

Traditional

Traditional

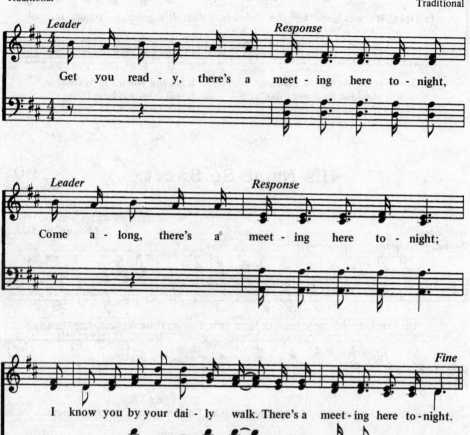

Get you read - y, there's a meet - ing here to - night,

Come a - long, there's a meet - ing here to - night;

I know you by your dai - ly walk. There's a meet - ing here to - night.

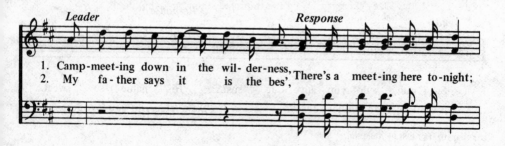

1. Camp - meet - ing down in the wil - der - ness,
2. My fa - ther says it is the bes',
There's a meet - ing here to - night;

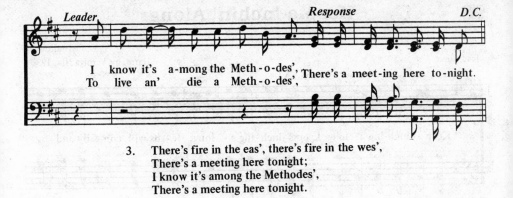

I   know it's   a-mong the Meth-o-des', There's a meet-ing here to-night.
To   live   an'   die   a   Meth-o-des',

3.   There's fire in the eas', there's fire in the wes',
     There's a meeting here tonight;
     I know it's among the Methodes',
     There's a meeting here tonight.

Freedom Train a-Comin'   92

Traditional   Traditional

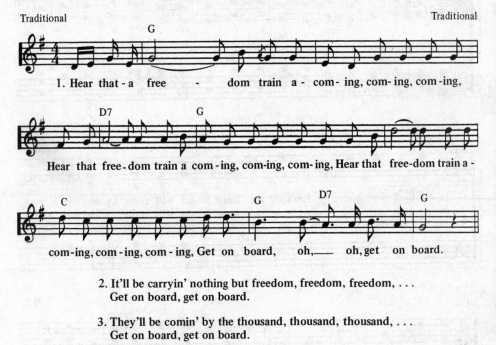

1. Hear that-a free - dom train a - com- ing, com- ing, com-ing,

Hear that free-dom train a com-ing, com-ing, com-ing, Hear that free-dom train a-

com-ing, com-ing, com-ing, Get on board, oh,— oh, get on board.

2. It'll be carryin' nothing but freedom, freedom, freedom, . . .
     Get on board, get on board.

3. They'll be comin' by the thousand, thousand, thousand, . . .
     Get on board, get on board.

4. It'll be carryin' freedom fighters, fighters, fighters, . . .
     Get on board, get on board.

5. It'll be carryin' registered voters, voters, voters, . . .
     Get on board, get on board.

6. It'll be rollin' through Mississippi, Mississippi, Mississippi, . . .
     Get on board, get on board.

93 Keep a-Inchin' Along

Traditional

Traditional
Harm. by Verolga Nix, 1933-

Keep a-inch-ing a-long, keep a-inch-ing a-long, Je-sus will come by and by.

Keep a-inch-ing a-long, like a poor inch-worm, Je-sus will come by and by.

Leader *Response* *Leader*

1. It was inch by inch that I sought the Lord, Je-sus will come by and by; It was
2. We'll inch and inch and inch a-long, Je-sus will come by and by; And
3. Oh, trials and trou-bles on the way, Je-sus will come by and by; But

Response *D.S.*

inch by inch that He saved my soul, Je-sus will come by and by. Keep a-
inch by inch till we get home, Je-sus will come by and by. Keep a-
we must watch as well as pray, Je-sus will come by and by. Keep a-

Little David, Play on Your Harp

Traditional

Traditional

Refrain
With spirit

Lit - tle Da - vid, play on your harp, Hal - le - lu! Hal - le -

lu! Lit - tle Da - vid, play on your harp, Hal - le - lu! Lit - tle Da - vid, lu!

Unison

1. Lit - tle Da - vid was a shep - herd boy, He
2. Josh - u - a was the son of Nun, He
3. Done told you once, done told you twice, There're

killed Go - li - ath and shout - ed for joy.
nev - er would quit till the work was done.
sin - ners in hell for shoot - ing dice.

95 I Want Jesus to Walk with Me

Traditional
Harm. by J. Jefferson Cleveland, 1937-
and Verolga Nix, 1933-

Traditional

1. I want Je - sus to walk with me; I want Je - sus to walk with me; All a - long my pil - grim jour - ney, Lord, I want Je - sus to walk with me.
2. In my tri - als, Lord, walk with me; In my tri - als, Lord, walk with me; When my heart is al - most break - ing, Lord, I want Je - sus to walk with me.
3. When I'm in trou - ble, Lord, walk with me; When I'm in trou - ble, Lord, walk with me; When my head is bowed in sor - row, Lord, I want Je - sus to walk with me.

Traditional   Traditional

Peter, Go Ring Them Bells

Traditional

Traditional

Refrain

Oh, Pe - ter, go ring them bells, Pe - ter, go ring them bells,

Pe - ter, go ring them bells, I heard from heav - en to - day. I

heard from heav - en to - day, I heard from heav-en to - day, (1.) I
(2-3.) It's
(4-5.) He's

Fine

thank God, and I thank you, too,
good news, and I thank you, too, I heard from heav - en to - day.
gone where E - li - jah has gone,

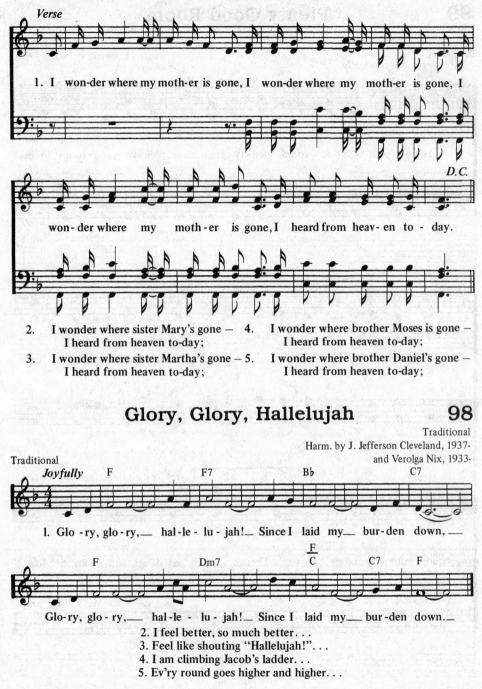

Verse

1. I won-der where my moth-er is gone, I won-der where my moth-er is gone, I

won-der where my moth-er is gone, I heard from heav-en to-day.

D.C.

2. I wonder where sister Mary's gone —
   I heard from heaven to-day;
3. I wonder where sister Martha's gone —
   I heard from heaven to-day;
4. I wonder where brother Moses is gone —
   I heard from heaven to-day;
5. I wonder where brother Daniel's gone —
   I heard from heaven to-day;

Glory, Glory, Hallelujah 98

Traditional
Harm. by J. Jefferson Cleveland, 1937-
and Verolga Nix, 1933-

Traditional

Joyfully   F   F7   Bb   C7

1. Glo-ry, glo-ry,— hal-le-lu-jah!— Since I laid my— bur-den down,—

F   Dm7   F/C   C7   F

Glo-ry, glo-ry,— hal-le-lu-jah!— Since I laid my— bur-den down.—

2. I feel better, so much better...
3. Feel like shouting "Hallelujah!"...
4. I am climbing Jacob's ladder...
5. Ev'ry round goes higher and higher...

99   Plenty Good Room

Traditional

Traditional
Arr. by Fredricka R. Young, 1928-

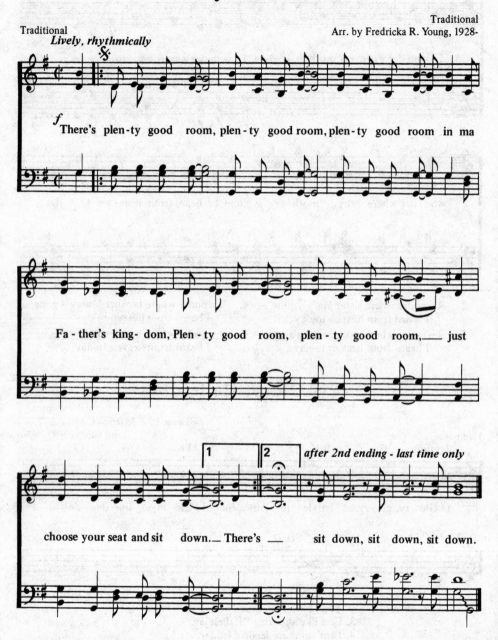

Lively, rhythmically

f There's plen-ty good room, plen-ty good room, plen-ty good room in ma

Fa-ther's king-dom, Plen-ty good room, plen-ty good room,___ just

| 1 | 2 | *after 2nd ending - last time only* |

choose your seat and sit down.___ There's ___ sit down, sit down, sit down.

Solo *slowly*

mf

1. I would not be a sin - ner,— I'll tell you the rea - son why;—
2. I would not be a li - ar,— I'll tell you the rea - son why;—
3. I would not be a cheat - er,— I'll tell you the rea - son why;—

p Hum_____ Hum_____

I'm a - fraid my Lord might call on__ me,__ and I

Hum_____

would - n't be read - y to die._____ There's-a

a tempo

Hum_____ There's

100
Hush, Hush,
Somebody's Callin' Mah Name

Traditional

Traditional
Harm. and notation by
J. Jefferson Cleveland, 1937-
and Verolga Nix, 1933-

Unison - unaccompanied, with a rhythmic feeling and mood

The "free" or added responses of (Hum) and (Thank You, Jesus) may be done by one or more voices to help set the mood and keep the rhythm.

Arr. copyright ©1979 by Abingdon.

* other verses may be added:

I'm so glad. Trou-ble don't last al - ways, yea, yea, yea.

I'm so glad. Trou-ble don't last al - ways. Oh mah Lawd,

Oh mah Lawd - ie, what shall I do?

2. Sounds like Jesus. Somebody's callin' mah name, . . .
3. Soon one mornin', death'll come creepin' in mah room, . . .
4. I'm so glad. Ah got mah religion in time, . . .
5. I'm so glad. I'm on mah journey home, . . .

He Nevuh Said a Mumbalin' Word   101

Slowly and reverently   Traditional

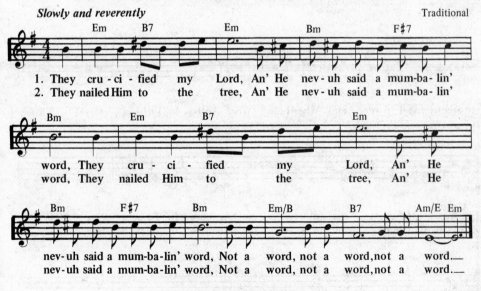

1. They cru - ci - fied my Lord, An' He nev-uh said a mum-ba-lin'
2. They nailed Him to the tree, An' He nev-uh said a mum-ba-lin'

word, They cru - ci - fied my Lord, An' He
word, They nailed Him to the tree, An' He

nev-uh said a mum-ba-lin' word, Not a word, not a word,not a word.
nev-uh said a mum-ba-lin' word, Not a word, not a word,not a word.

3. They pierced Him in the side, . . .
4. The blood came streamin' down, . . .
5. He hung His head and died, . . .

102   Oh, Freedom

Traditional

Traditional
Arr. by J. Jefferson Cleveland, 1937 -
and Verolga Nix, 1933 -

1. Oh,_____ free-dom! Oh,_____ free-dom! Oh,_____ free-dom all o-ver me! When I am free! An'be- fo' I'd be a slave, I'll be

1. Oh,_____ free-dom! Oh,_____ free-dom! Oh,_____ free-dom o-ver me! (o - ver me!) An'be – fo' I'd be a slave, I'll be
2. No mo' moan-in', no mo' moan-in', no mo' moan-in' o-ver me! (o - ver me!) An'be – fo' I'd be a slave, I'll be

bur-ied in my grave, An' go home to my Lord an' be free.

bur-ied in my grave, An' go home to my Lord an' be free.
bur-ied in my grave, An' go home to my Lord an' be free.

3. No mo' weepin', . . .   5. There'll be shoutin', . . .
4. There'll be singin', . . .   6. There'll be prayin', . . .

Rockin' Jerusalem 103

Traditional   Traditional

Refrain
Leader   *Response*   *All*   1   2

O Mar-y, O Mar-tha, O Mar-y, ring dem bells. ring dem bells. I hear arch-

an-gels a-rock-in' Je-ru-sa-lem, I hear arch-an-gels a-ring-in' dem bells. *Fine*

Verses
Leader   *Response*

1. Church get-tin' high-er! Rock-in' Je-ru-sa-lem!
2. Lis-ten to the lambs!__
3. New Je-ru-sa-lem!__

Leader   *Response*   D.C.

Church get-tin' high-er! Ring-in' dem bells.
Lis-ten to the lambs!__
New Je-ru-sa-lem!__

104 Swing Low, Sweet Chariot

Traditional   Traditional

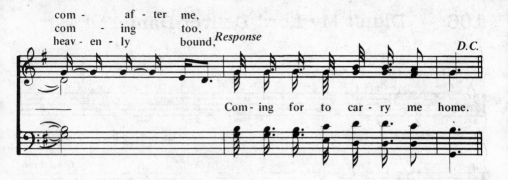

com - af - ter me,
com - ing too,
heav - en - ly bound, *Response*

D.C.

Com - ing for to car - ry me home.

Mah God Is So High
105

Traditional

Traditional

% *Refrain*

Mah God is so high,__ yuh can't get o - ver Him; He's

so low,__ yuh can't git un - der Him; He's so wide,___ yuh

Fine

can't get a - roun' Him; Yuh mus' come in__ by an through de Lam'. He's

Verses

1. One day as I was a - walk - in' a - long de Heb-en-ly road, Mah
2. I'll take mah gos - pel trum - pet an' I'll be - gin to blow, An'

D.S.

Sav - ior spoke un - to me an' He fill mah heart_ wid His love. Mah God is
if mah Sav - ior help me I'll blow wher-ev - er I__ go. Mah God is

Didn't My Lord Deliver Daniel?

Traditional   Traditional

Refrain Unison or Parts

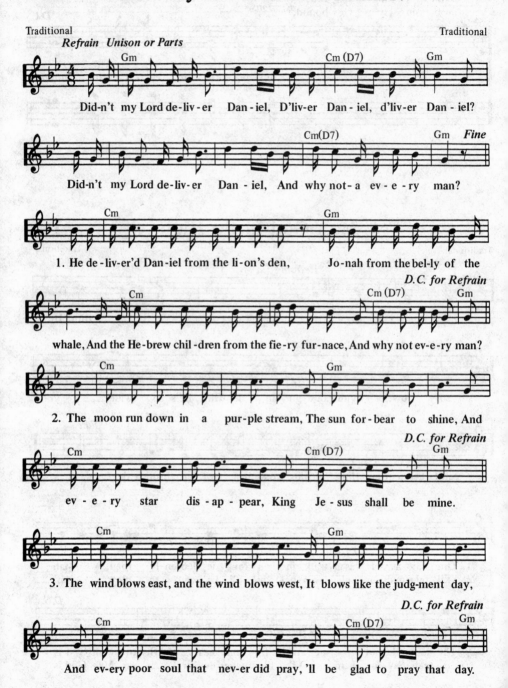

Did-n't my Lord de-liv-er Dan-iel, D'liv-er Dan-iel, d'liv-er Dan-iel?

Did-n't my Lord de-liv-er Dan-iel, And why not-a ev-e-ry man?

1. He de-liv-er'd Dan-iel from the li-on's den, Jo-nah from the bel-ly of the

D.C. for Refrain

whale, And the He-brew chil-dren from the fie-ry fur-nace, And why not ev-e-ry man?

2. The moon run down in a pur-ple stream, The sun for-bear to shine, And

D.C. for Refrain

ev-e-ry star dis-ap-pear, King Je-sus shall be mine.

3. The wind blows east, and the wind blows west, It blows like the judg-ment day,

D.C. for Refrain

And ev-ery poor soul that nev-er did pray, 'll be glad to pray that day.

4. I set my foot on the Gos-pel ship, And the ship it be-gin to sail,

D.C. for Refrain

It land-ed me o-ver on Ca-naan's shore, And I'll nev-er come back an-y more.

Hard Trials

107

Traditional
Arr. by J. Jefferson Cleveland, 1937-
and Verolga Nix, 1933-

Traditional

Lively
unison

1. The fox - es, they have holes in the ground, The birds have nests in the air,

The Chris-tians have a hid - ing place, But sin - ners ain't got no - where.

Refrain

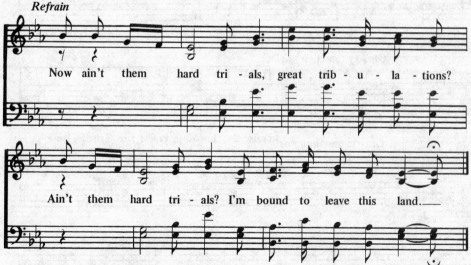

Now ain't them hard tri - als, great trib - u - la - tions?

Ain't them hard tri - als? I'm bound to leave this land.___

2. Oh, Methodist, Methodist is my name,
   Methodist till I die,
   Been baptized on the Methodist side,
   And a Methodist will I die.

3. Oh, Baptist, Baptist is my name,
   Baptist till I die,
   Been baptized on the Baptist side,
   And a Baptist will I die.

108 Live a-Humble

Traditional

Traditional
Harm. by J. Jefferson Cleveland, 1937-

Joyfully

Live a - hum - ble,___ hum - ble,___ Hum - ble your - selves, the

1. **2.** *Fine*

Glo - ry and hon - or!___

bell's done rung, Live a - bell's done rung. Glo - ry and hon - or!___

Praise King

Praise King

Glo - ry and hon - or!

1. **2.** *D.S.*

Je - sus!

Glo - ry and hon - or! Praise the Lord! Praise the Lord! Live a -

Je - sus!

D.S.

1. Watch that sun, how stead-y it runs, Don't let it catch you with your work un-done. Live a -

2. Ev-er see such a man as God? He gave up His Son for to come and die.

D.S.

Gave up His Son for to come and die, Just to save my soul from a burn-ing fire, Live a -

Dedicated to Dr. J. deKoven Killingsworth,
Music Professor Emeritus, Clark College, Atlanta, Georgia

Jubilee

109

Traditional
Arr. by J. Jefferson Cleveland, 1937-

Traditional

March tempo, with spirit

Women

Ju-bi - lee, Ju-bi-lee, O____ Lord - y, Ju-bi-lee, Ju-bi-lee,

Men

Solo or unison

┌─3─┐

1. What is the mat-ter, the church won't shout?
My Lord, Ju-bi-lee 2. What is the mat-ter with the mourn - er? O____
3. What is the mat-ter, the church won't move?

Solo or unison

1. Some-bod-y in there that ought-a be out!
Lord-y. 2. The dev-il's in the "a - men cor - ner"! My Lord, Ju-bi-lee.
3. Some-bod-y in there that's car-ryin' bad news!

Standin' in the Need of Prayer

Traditional   *Leader*   Traditional

1. Not my broth - er, nor my sis - ter, but it's me, O Lord,
2. Not the preach - er, nor the dea - con, but it's me, O Lord,
3. Not my fa - ther, nor my moth - er, but it's me, O Lord,
4. Not the stran - ger, nor my neigh - bor, but it's me, O Lord,

Response   *Leader*

Stand - in' in the need of prayer; Not my broth - er, nor my sis - ter,
Stand - in' in the need of prayer; Not the preach - er, nor the dea - con,
Stand - in' in the need of prayer; Not my fa - ther, nor my moth - er,
Stand - in' in the need of prayer; Not the stran - ger, nor my neigh - bor,

                                   Response

but it's me, O Lord, Stand - in' in the need of prayer.
but it's me, O Lord, Stand - in' in the need of prayer.
but it's me, O Lord, Stand - in' in the need of prayer.
but it's me, O Lord, Stand - in' in the need of prayer.

All

It's me, It's me, it's me, O Lord, Stand - in' in the need of prayer;

It's me, It's me, it's me, O Lord, Stand-in' in the need of prayer.
It's me,

Trampin'

111

Traditional
Arr. by J. Jefferson Cleveland, 1937-
and Verolga Nix, 1933-

Traditional

Slowly, with a firm beat

I'm tramp-in', tramp-in', Try'n' to make Heav-en ma home.

I'm tramp-in', tramp-in', Try'n' to make Heav-en ma home,

Hal-le-lu-jah, I'm a-tramp-in,' tramp-in', Try'n' to make Heav-en ma home.

Fine

I'm tramp-in', tramp-in', Try'n' to make Heav-en ma home.

women *men*

1. I've nev-er been to Heav-en, but I've been tol' Try'n' to make Heav-en ma home.
2. If you git dere be-fo' I do

women *men* *D.C.*

1. Dat de streets up dere are paved wid gol'. Try'n' to make Heav-en ma home.
2. Tell all ma friends I'm com-ing too.

112 Go Down, Moses

Traditional

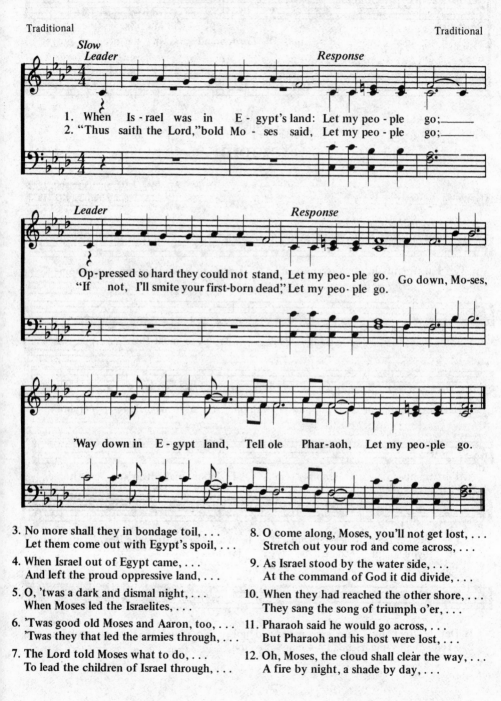

Slow

Leader ... **Response**

1. When Is - rael was in E - gypt's land: Let my peo - ple go;____
2. "Thus saith the Lord,"bold Mo - ses said, Let my peo - ple go;____

Leader ... **Response**

Op-pressed so hard they could not stand, Let my peo-ple go. Go down, Mo-ses,
"If not, I'll smite your first-born dead," Let my peo-ple go.

'Way down in E - gypt land, Tell ole Phar-aoh, Let my peo-ple go.

3. No more shall they in bondage toil, . . .
   Let them come out with Egypt's spoil, . . .

4. When Israel out of Egypt came, . . .
   And left the proud oppressive land, . . .

5. O, 'twas a dark and dismal night, . . .
   When Moses led the Israelites, . . .

6. 'Twas good old Moses and Aaron, too, . . .
   'Twas they that led the armies through, . . .

7. The Lord told Moses what to do, . . .
   To lead the children of Israel through, . . .

8. O come along, Moses, you'll not get lost, . . .
   Stretch out your rod and come across, . . .

9. As Israel stood by the water side, . . .
   At the command of God it did divide, . . .

10. When they had reached the other shore, . . .
    They sang the song of triumph o'er, . . .

11. Pharaoh said he would go across, . . .
    But Pharaoh and his host were lost, . . .

12. Oh, Moses, the cloud shall clear the way, . . .
    A fire by night, a shade by day, . . .

13. You'll not get lost in the wilderness, . . .
   With a lighted candle in your breast, . . .

14. Jordan shall stand up like a wall, . . .
   And the walls of Jericho shall fall, . . .

15. Your foes shall not before you stand, . . .
   And you'll possess fair Canaan's land, . . .

16. 'Twas just about in harvest-time, . . .
   When Joshua led his host divine, . . .

17. Oh, let us all from bondage flee, . . .
   And let us all in Christ be free, . . .

18. We need not always weep and moan, . . .
   And wear these slavery chains forlorn, . . .

De Ol' Ark's a-Moverin'

113

Traditional
Arr. by J. Jefferson Cleveland, 1937-

Traditional

Oh, de ol' ark's a-mov-er-in', a-mov-er-in', a-mov-er-in', De

ol' ark's a-mov-er-in' an' I'm a-goin' home. I'm goin' home.

Solo or Unison

1. See dat sis-tuh dressed so fine?
2. See dat brud-der dressed so gay?
3. Ol' ark she reel, Ol' ark rock,

She ain't got re-li-gion on-a her min'.
Sa-tan goin' come an' car-ry him a-way.
Ol' ark land-ed on de moun-tain-top.

114 Ain't Dat Good News?

Traditional

Traditional
Arr. by J. Jefferson Cleveland, 1937-

Spirited

Leader

1. Got a crown up in de King-dom, ain't dat good news?
2. Got a harp up in de King-dom, ain't dat good news?
3. Got a robe up in de King-dom, ain't dat good news?
4. Got a slip-pers in de King-dom, ain't dat good news?
5. Got a Sav-ior in de King-dom, ain't dat good news?

Response

Leader

Got a crown up in de
Got a harp up in de
Got a robe up in de
Got a slip-pers in de
Got a Sav-ior in de

Response

King-dom, ain't dat good news?

All

I'm a-goin' to lay down dis world, Goin' to shoul-der up mah

cross, Goin' to take it home to Je-sus, ain't dat good news?

In memory of my sister, Ms. Shirley Y. Cleveland

Deep River

Traditional

Traditional
Arr. by J. Jefferson Cleveland, 1937-

116 De Gospel Train

Traditional

Traditional

Lively

Git on board, lit-tle chil-dren, Git on board, lit-tle chil-dren,

Fine

Git on board, lit-tle chil-dren, Dere's room for man-y a mo'.

Solo or Unison

1. De Gos - pel train's a - com - in', I hear it jus' at han',
2. I hear de train a - com - in', She's com - in' roun' de curve,
3. De fare is cheap an' all can go, De rich an' poor are dere,

D.C.

I hear de car wheels rum - blin', An' roll - in' thro' de lan'.
She's loos-ened all her steam an' brakes, An' strain- in' eb - 'ry nerve.
No sec - ond class a - board dis train, No dif - f'rence in de fare.

Roll, Jordan, Roll

Traditional   Traditional

Refrain

Roll, Jor-dan, roll,   roll, Jor-dan, roll,   I want to go to heav-en when I die, To

Fine   *Verse*

hear Jor-dan roll.   1. Oh,   broth-ers, you ought   t'have been there, Yes, my

D.C.

Lord!   A sit-ting in   the King-dom, To   hear Jor-dan roll.

2. Oh, preachers, you ought t'have been there, . . .
3. Oh, sinners, you ought, . . .
4. Oh, mourners, you ought, . . .
5. Oh, seekers, you ought, . . .
6. Oh, mothers, you ought, . . .
7. Oh, sisters, you ought, . . .

118 Changed Mah Name

Traditional

Traditional
Arr. by Verolga Nix, 1933-

Solemnly (solo or unison)

1. Ah tol'__ Je-sus it would be all right,__ if He changed mah name.__
2. Je - sus__tol' me ah would have to live hum-ble, if He changed mah name.__
3. Je - sus__tol' me that the world would be 'gainst me, if He changed mah name.__
4. But ah tol' Je-sus It would be all right__ if He changed mah name.__

__ Ah tol'__ Je-sus it would be__ all right__ if He changed mah name.__
__ Je - sus__ tol' me ah would have to live hum-ble if He changed mah name.__
__ Je - sus__ tol' me the world would be 'gainst me if He changed mah name.__
__ But ah tol' Je-sus it would be__ all right__ if He changed mah name.__

__ Ah tol'__ Je - sus it would be__ all right,__ if He
__ Je - sus__ tol' me ah would have to live hum - ble if He
__ Je - sus__ tol' me the world world would be 'gainst me if He
__ But ah tol' Je - sus it would be__ all right,__ if He

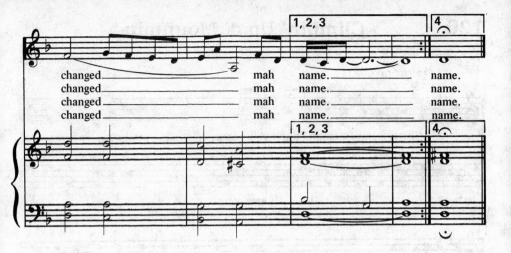

changed_____ mah name._____ name.
changed_____ mah name._____ name.
changed_____ mah name._____ name.
changed_____ mah name._____ name.

Do, Lord, Remember Me 119

Traditional

Traditional

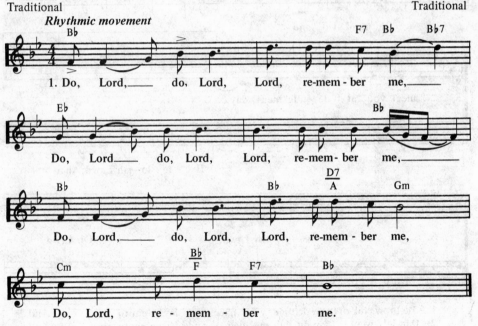

1. Do, Lord,_____ do, Lord, Lord, re-mem-ber me,_____
Do, Lord_____ do, Lord, Lord, re-mem-ber me,_____
Do, Lord,_____ do, Lord, Lord, re-mem-ber me,
Do, Lord, re - mem - ber me.

2. When I'm in trouble, Lord, remember me.
3. When I'm dyin', Lord, remember me.
4. When this world's on fire, Lord, remember me.

120   Climbin' Up d' Mountain

Traditional

Traditional
Arr. by Verolga Nix, 1933-

Climb-in' up d' moun-tain, chil - dren.   Did-n't come here for to

Good Lawd, Ah

stay,   If ah nev-er-more see you a - gain, gon-na

Oh, my Lawd, and

meet you at de judg-ment day.___

Hal - le - lu - jah, Lawd, Ah'm

Oh, Lawd,   *Oh, Lawd,*

1. He-brew chil-dren in de fier - y fur-nace. And dey be-gin to pray,   And de
2. Dan-iel went in de li-ons' den,__ And he be-gin to pray,   And de

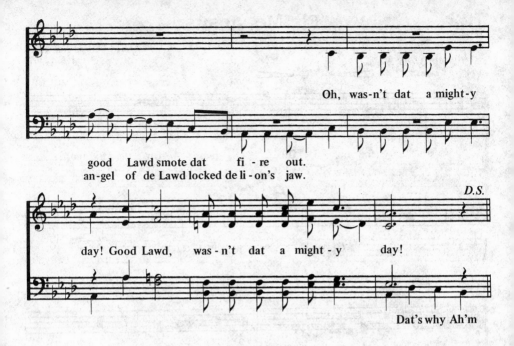

Oh, was-n't dat a might-y

good Lawd smote dat fi - re out.
an-gel of de Lawd locked de li - on's jaw.

day! Good Lawd, was-n't dat a might-y day!

D.S.

Dat's why Ah'm

Ev'ry Time I Feel the Spirit 121

Traditional

Traditional

Fast *Refrain* *Fine*

Ev-'ry time I feel the Spir-it mov-ing in my heart, I will pray.

Solo or Unison

Cm

Bb7

Eb *D.C.*

1. Up-on the moun-tain my Lord spoke, Out His mouth came fire and smoke.
   All a-round me looks so shine, Ask my Lord if all was mine.
2. Jor-dan Riv-er is chil-ly and cold, Chills the bod-y but not the soul.
   Ain't but one train on dis track, Runs to heav-en and right back.

122 Fix Me, Jesus

Traditional

Traditional
Arr. by Verolga Nix, 1933-

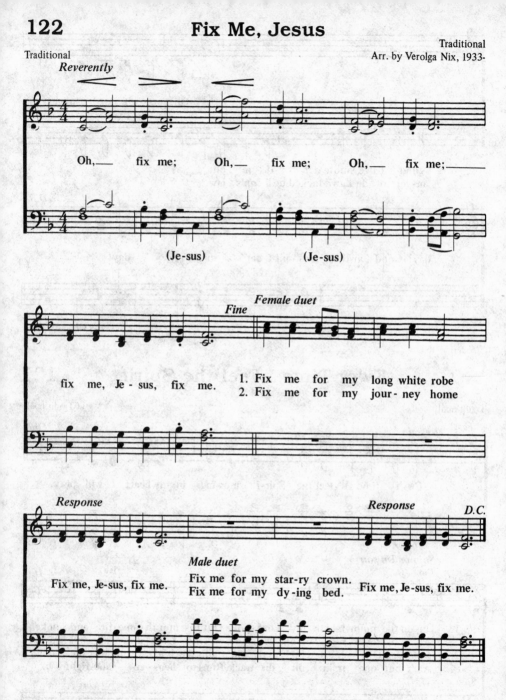

Reverently

Oh,— fix me; Oh,— fix me; Oh,— fix me;—

(Je-sus) (Je-sus)

Fine **Female duet**

fix me, Je-sus, fix me.

1. Fix me for my long white robe
2. Fix me for my jour-ney home

Response *Response* *D.C.*

Fix me, Je-sus, fix me.

Male duet

Fix me for my star-ry crown.
Fix me for my dy-ing bed.

Fix me, Je-sus, fix me.

Balm in Gilead

Harm. by Verolga Nix

Slowly

There is a balm in Gil - e - ad, to make the wound-ed whole,

There is a balm in Gil - e - ad, to heal the sin - sick soul, soul.

Leader

1. Some - times I feel dis - cour - aged, And think my work's in vain,
2. Don't ev - er feel dis - cour - aged, For Je - sus is your friend,
3. If you can - not preach like Pe - ter, If you can - not pray like Paul,

Response   D.S.

But then the Ho - ly Spir - it Re - vives my soul a - gain. There is a
And if you look for knowl-edge, He'll ne'er re - fuse to lend. There is a
you can tell the love of Je - sus, And say "He died for all." There is a

124 Good News

Traditional

Traditional

Lively

Good news! The char-i-ot's com-ing. Good news! The char-i-ot's com-ing. Good

news! The char-i-ot's com-ing, And I don't want it to leave-a me be-hind.

Fine

1. There's a long white robe in the heav-en, I know_____

A long white robe in the heav-en, I know.

1. There's a long white robe in the heav-en, I know_____

A long white robe in the heav-en, I know.

D.C.

There's a long white robe in the heav-en, I know, And I don't want it to leave me be-hind.

2. pair of wings . . .   3. pair of shoes . . .   4. starry crown . . .   5. golden harp . . .

You'd Better Min'

Traditional
Harm. by J. Jefferson Cleveland, 1937-

Traditional

Leader

1. You'd bet-ter min' how you talk, you'd bet-ter min'what you talk - in' a-bout,
2. You'd bet-ter min' how you sing, you'd bet-ter min'what you sing- in' a-bout,
3. You'd bet-ter min' how you shout,you'd bet-ter min' what you shout-in' a-bout,

Response

You got to give ac - count in de Judg-ment,you'd bet - ter min'.

You'd bet - ter min',   you'd bet - ter   min',_____

you'd bet - ter min',   you'd bet-ter min',

you got to give ac - count in de Judg-ment,you'd bet - ter min'.

126 Were You There?

Traditional
Harm. by J. Jefferson Cleveland, 1937-
and Verolga Nix, 1933-

Traditional

1. Were you there when they cru - ci - fied my Lord? (were you there?)
2. Were you there when they nailed Him to the tree? (to the tree?)
3. Were you there when they pierced Him in the side? (in the side?)
4. Were you there when the sun re - fused to shine? (were you there?)
5. Were you there when they laid Him in the tomb? (in the tomb?)

Were you there when they cru - ci - fied my Lord? Oh!_____
Were you there when they nailed Him to the tree? Oh!_____
Were you there when they pierced Him in the side? Oh!_____
Were you there when the sun re - fused to shine? Oh!_____
Were you there when they laid Him in the tomb? Oh!_____

rit.

Some - times it caus - es me to trem - ble, trem - ble, trem - ble.
Some - times it caus - es me to trem - ble, trem - ble, trem - ble.
Some - times it caus - es me to trem - ble, trem - ble, trem - ble.
Some - times it caus - es me to trem - ble, trem - ble, trem - ble.
Some - times it caus - es me to trem - ble, trem - ble, trem - ble.

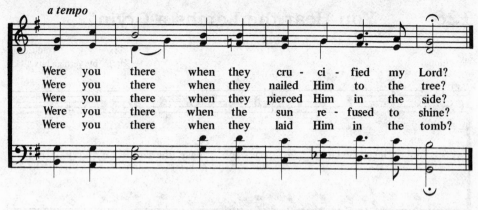

a tempo

Were	you	there	when	they	cru - ci - fied	my	Lord?
Were	you	there	when	they	nailed Him	to	the	tree?
Were	you	there	when	they	pierced Him	in	the	side?
Were	you	there	when	the	sun re - fused	to	shine?
Were	you	there	when	they	laid Him	in	the	tomb?

We Shall Overcome

127

Traditional
Harm. by J. Jefferson Cleveland, 1937-

Traditional

1. We shall o - ver - come,____ We shall o - ver - come,____
We shall o - ver - come some - day._____ Oh,____
If in our hearts we do be - lieve, We shall o - ver - come some - day.____

2. We'll walk hand in hand . . .   4. We are not afraid . . .
3. We shall all have peace . . .   5. God is on our side . . .

128 You Hear the Lambs a-Cryin'

Traditional

Traditional
Harm. by Verolga Nix 1933-

You hear the lambs a - cry - in', hear the lambs a cry - in',

hear the lambs a - cry - in', O Shep-herd, feed my sheep. You feed my sheep.

Leader
My Sav-ior spoke these words so sweet, *Response*

Leader
say-in',

Oo_____ O Shep-herd, feed my sheep,

"Pe - ter, if you love me, feed my sheep." *Response*   D.S.

Oo_____ O Shep-herd, feed my sheep. You

2. Lord, I love Thee, Thou dost know;
    Response: O Shepherd, feed my sheep.
    O give me grace to love Thee more.
    Response: O Shepherd, feed my sheep.

3. Wasn't that an awful shame?
    Response: O Shepherd, feed my sheep.
    He hung three hours in mortal pain.
    Response: O Shepherd, feed my sheep.

Wade in the Water   129

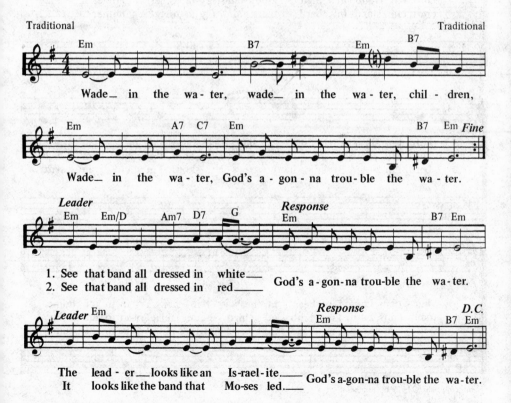

Traditional   Traditional

Wade— in the wa-ter, wade— in the wa-ter, chil-dren,

Wade— in the wa-ter, God's a-gon-na trou-ble the wa-ter.

Leader   *Response*

1. See that band all dressed in white___
2. See that band all dressed in red___
God's a-gon-na trou-ble the wa-ter.

Leader   *Response*   D.C.

The   lead-er___looks like an   Is-rael-ite.___
It   looks like the band that   Mo-ses led.___
God's a-gon-na trou-ble the wa-ter.

130

Tryin' to Get Home

Traditional
Harm. by J. Jefferson Cleveland, 1937-
and Verolga Nix, 1933-

Traditional

1. Lord, I'm bear-in' heav-y bur-dens, Try-in' to get home;_____
2. Lord, I'm climb-in' high moun-tains, Try-in' to get home;_____
3. Lord, I'm stand-in' hard tri-als, Try-in' to get home;_____

Lord, I'm bear-in' heav-y bur-dens, Try-in' to get home;_____
Lord, I'm climb-in' high moun-tains, Try-in' to get home;_____
Lord, I'm stand-in' hard tri-als, Try-in' to get home;_____

Lord, I'm bear-in' heav-y bur-dens, Lord, I'm bear-in' heav-y
Lord, I'm climb-in' high moun-tains, Lord, I'm climb-in' high
Lord, I'm stand-in' hard tri-als, Lord, I'm stand-in' hard

bur-dens, Lord, I'm bear-in' heav-y bur-dens, Try-in' to get home.
moun-tains, Lord, I'm climb-in' high moun-tains, Try-in' to get home.
tri-als, Lord, I'm stand-in' hard tri-als, Try-in' to get home.

Traditional   Traditional

'Tis the old ship of Zi - on, 'Tis the old ship of Zi - on,

Fine

'Tis the old ship of Zi - on, Git on board, git on board.

Leader   *Response*

1. It has land-ed many a thou-sand, It has land-ed many a thou-sand,
2. Ain't no dan-ger in de wa - ter, Ain't no dan-ger in de wa - ter,

D.C.

It has land-ed many a thou-sand,
Ain't no dan-ger in de wa - ter,   Git on board, Git on board.

3. It was good for my dear mother, . . .
4. It was good for my dear father, . . .
5. It will take you home to Glory, . . .

132 This Little Light of Mine

Traditional
Arr. by J. Jefferson Cleveland, 1937-
and Verolga Nix, 1933-

Traditional

2. Everywhere I go, . . .
3. All through the night, . . .

The Time for Praying

133

Traditional

Traditional
Arr. by Verolga Nix, 1933-

Steal Away

Traditional

Traditional

Slowly with feeling

Response

Steal a-way, steal a-way, steal a-way to Je-sus!

Steal a-way, steal a-way home, I ain't got long to stay here!

Leader

1. My Lord calls me, He calls me by the thun-der;
2. Green trees are bend-ing, Poor sin-ner stands a-trem-bling;
3. Tomb-stones are burst-ing, Poor sin-ner stands a-trem-bling;
4. My Lord calls me, He calls me by the light-ning,

Response

The trum-pet sounds with-in-a my soul, I ain't got long to stay here.

Fine

D.C.

City Called Heaven

Traditional

Traditional

1. I am a poor pil - grim of sor - row,— I'm tossed in this
2. My moth-er has reached that pure glo - ry,— My fa-ther's still

wide world a - lone,— No hope__ have I for to -
walk - in' in sin,____ My broth - ers and sis - ters won't

mor - row,— I've start - ed to make heav'n my home. Some -
own me,— Be - cause I am tryin' to get in. Some -

times I am tossed__ and driv - en,— Lord, Some - times I don't

know where to roam,_____ I've heard of a

cit - y called heav - en,— I've start-ed to make it my home.

136 Come Out de Wilderness

Traditional   Traditional

1. Tell me, how did you feel when you
2. Well, I loved ev-'ry-bod-y when I come out de wil-der-ness,
3. Well, my soul was so hap-py when I

come out de wil-der-ness, come out de wil-der-ness?

Leader   **Response**

How did you feel when you
Loved ev-'ry-bod-y when I come out de wil-der-ness?
Soul was so hap-py when I

Refrain

Lean-ing on de Lord, I'm a lean-ing on de Lord,

I'm a lean - ing on de Lord, I'm a -

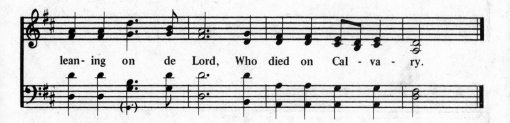

lean - ing on de Lord, Who died on Cal - va - ry.

Many Thousand Gone 137

Traditional   Traditional

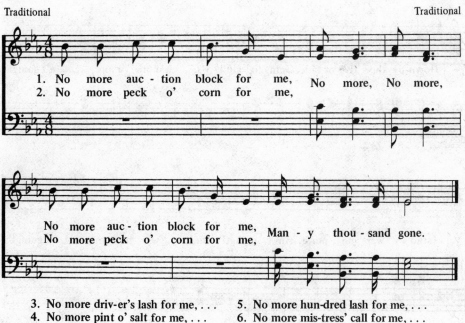

1. No more auc - tion block for me, No more, No more,
2. No more peck o' corn for me,

No more auc - tion block for me, Man - y thou - sand gone.
No more peck o' corn for me,

3. No more driv-er's lash for me, . . .   5. No more hun-dred lash for me, . . .
4. No more pint o' salt for me, . . .   6. No more mis-tress' call for me, . . .

Study War No More

Traditional

Traditional

Lively

Going to lay down my sword and shield, Down by the riv-er-side, Down by the

riv-er-side, Down by the riv-er-side; Going to lay down my sword and shield,

Down by the riv-er-side, Going to stud-y war no more.__ I ain't goingt'

stud-y war no more, Ain't goingt' stud-y war no more, Ain't goingt'

stud - y war no more,_____ Ain't goingt' stud- y war no

stud - y war no more, I ain't goingt'

more, Ain't goingt' stud-y war no more, Ain't goingt' stud- y___ war no more.___

2. Going to lay down my burden,
   Down by the riverside, . . .

3. Going to try on my starry crown,
   Down by the riverside, . . .

4. Going to meet my dear old father,
   Down by the riverside, . . .

5. Going to meet my dear old mother;
   Down by the riverside, . . .

6. Going to meet my loving Jesus,
   Down by the riverside, . . .

Kum Ba Yah, My Lord 139

Traditional   Traditional

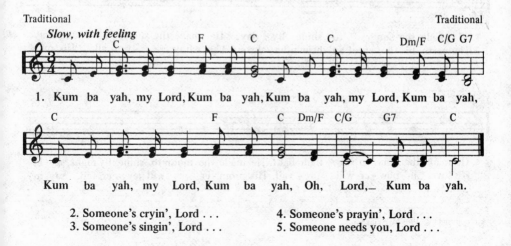

Slow, with feeling

1. Kum ba yah, my Lord, Kum ba yah, Kum ba yah, my Lord, Kum ba yah,

Kum ba yah, my Lord, Kum ba yah, Oh, Lord,_ Kum ba yah.

2. Someone's cryin', Lord . . .

3. Someone's singin', Lord . . .

4. Someone's prayin', Lord . . .

5. Someone needs you, Lord . . .

140

Dedicated to my mother, Mrs. Ida A. Nix

God Is a God

Traditional

Traditional
Arr. by Verolga Nix, 1933-

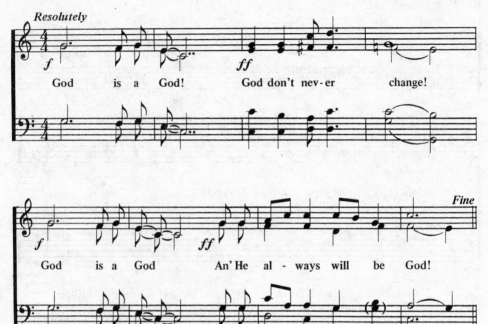

God   is   a   God!   God don't nev-er   change!

God   is   a   God   An' He al - ways will   be   God!

Unison or Solo

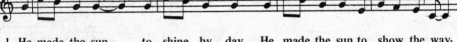

1. He made the sun   to shine by day, He made the sun to show the way,
2. The earth his foot-stool an' heav'n his throne, The whole cre - a - tion all   His own,

D.C.

He made the stars to show their light, He made the moon to shine by night, say-in'
His love an' pow - er will   pre - vail, His prom - is - es will nev - er fail,   say-in'

No Hidin' Place

Traditional

Traditional
Arr. by J. Jefferson Cleveland, 1937-

With fervor

1. Dere's no hid-in' place down dere, Dere's no hid-in' place down dere.

Solo, selected voices or unison

Oh, I went to the rock to hide my face, The

Oh, I (Hum)

rock cried out, "No hid - in' place"; Dere's no hid - in' place down dere.

no hid - in' place down dere.

2. Oh, de rock cried, "I'm burnin' too,"
   Oh, de rock cried, "I'm burnin' too,"
   Oh, de rock cried out, "I'm burnin' too,
   I want-a go to hebben as well as you."
   Dere's no hidin' place down dere.

3. Oh, de sinner-man he gambled an' fell,
   Oh, de sinner-man he gambled an' fell,
   Oh, de sinner-man gambled, he gambled
   an' fell,
   He wanted to go to hebben, but he had to go
   to hell.
   Dere's no hidin' place down dere.

142   Great Day

Traditional

Traditional
Harm. by J. Jefferson Cleveland, 1937-

Great day! Great day, the righ-teous march-ing. Great day.

1. Char - iot rode on the
2. This is the day of ____
3. We want no cow - ards ___
4. Going to take my breast-plate,

God's going to build up Zi - on's walls, Zi - on's walls.

moun-tain - top,	My God spoke and the
ju - bi - lee,	The Lord has set His ___
in our band,	We call for va - li - ant
sword, and shield, *Response*	And march out bold - ly ___

God's going to build up Zi - on's walls!

char - iot   did   stop,
peo - ple   free,
heart - ed   men,
in   the   field,

—   God's going   to   build   up   Zi - on's walls!

I've Been 'Buked   143

Traditional   Traditional

1. I've   been 'buked an' I've been scorned,_____
2. Dere   is   trou-ble all o - ver dis worl',_____
3. Ain'   gwine lay   my 'li - gion down,_____

I've   been 'buked an' I've been scorned, chil - dren.
Dere   is   trou-ble all o -ver dis worl', chil - dren.
Ain'   gwine lay   my 'li - gion down, chil - dren.

I've   been 'buked an' I've been scorned,_____
Dere   is   trou-ble all o-ver dis worl',_____
Ain'   gwine lay   my 'li - gion down,_____

I've   been talked a - bout sho's you' born.
Dere   is   trou- ble all o - ver dis worl'.
Ain'   gwine lay   my 'li - gion down.

144   I Been in de Storm So Long

Traditional   Traditional

Mournfully

I been in de storm so long, I been in de storm so long, chil - lun, I been in de storm so long, Oh, gim - me lit - tle time to pray.

1. I pray.

2. *Fine*

1. Oh, let me tell you, Moth - er, how I come 'long, Oh,
2. Now when I get to Heav - en I'll take my seat, Oh,

gim - me lit - tle time to pray, ____ With a hung down head and a
gim - me lit - tle time to pray, ____ An - a cast my crown at my

D.S. al Fine

ach - in' heart, Oh, gim - me lit - tle time to pray. 'Cause I
Je - sus' feet, Oh, gim - me lit - tle time to pray.

My Lord! What a Mourning

Traditional
Harm. by Verolga Nix, 1933-

Traditional

Refrain

My Lord! what a mourn-ing, My Lord! what a mourn-ing,— Yes,

Fine

My Lord! what a mourn-ing,— when the stars be-gin to fall.

Verses
Leader

1. You'll hear the trum-pet sound to wake the na-tions un-der-ground
2. You'll hear the sin-ner cry to wake the na-tions un-der-ground
3. You'll hear the Chris-tian shout to wake the na-tions un-der-ground

Response

D.C.

look-ing to my God's right hand
look-ing to my God's right hand   When the stars be-gin to fall.
look-ing to my God's right hand

146   Woke Up Dis Mornin'

Traditional

Traditional
Arr. by J. Jefferson Cleveland, 1937-
and Verolga Nix, 1933-

1. Oh, I woke up dis morn-in' wid mah min', An' it was stayed,

Response

Stayed on Je - sus,—

Woke up dis morn - in' wid mah min', An' it was stayed,

Stayed on Je - sus

Woke up dis morn - in' wid mah min', An' it was stayed,

Stayed on Je - sus,—

2. Can't hate your neighbor in your min', if you keep it stayed, . . .
3. Makes you love everybody with your min', when you keep it stayed, . . .
4. De devil can't catch you in your min', if you keep it stayed, . . .
5. Jesus is de captain in your min', when you keep it stayed, . . .

Amen

147

Traditional
Harm. by J. Jefferson Cleveland, 1937-
and Verolga Nix, 1933-

Traditional

A - men, A - men,
A - men, Oh, Lawd - y! A - men, Have mer - cy!

A - men, A - men, A - men. men.
A - men, A - men, A - men. Sing it o - ver now, men.

148   I Feel Like My Time Ain't Long

Traditional

Traditional
Harm. by J. Jefferson Cleveland, 1937-

Very rhythmic

I feel like, I feel like, I feel like my time ain't long,

Fine

I feel like, I feel like, I feel like my time ain't long.

Leader

1. Went to the grave - yard the oth - er day, I
2. Some - times I'm up, some - times I'm down, I
3. Better min', my broth - er, how you walk on the cross, I

Response   *Leader*

feel like my time ain't long, I look'd at the place where my
feel like my time ain't long, And some - times I'm al - most_
feel like my time ain't long, Your foot might slip and your

Response

D.C.

moth - er	lay,	I	feel like my time ain't	long.
on	the	ground,	I	feel like my time ain't	long.
soul	get	lost,	I	feel like my time ain't	long.

I Stood on de Ribber ob Jerdon   149

Traditional
Harm. by J. Jefferson Cleveland, 1937-
and Verolga Nix, 1933-

Traditional

1. I stood on de rib - ber ob Jer - don, to see dat ship come sail - in' o - ber;
stood on de rib - ber ob Jer - don, to see dat ship sail by.

O moan - er, don' ya weep, when ya see dat ship come sail - in' o - ber,

Shout "Glo - ry Hal - le - lu - jah!" When ya see dat ship sail by.

2. O sister, ya bettuh be ready
To see dat ship come sailin' ober;
Brother, ya bettuh be ready
To see dat ship sail by.

3. O preacher, ya bettuh be ready
To see dat ship come sailin' ober;
Deacon, ya bettuh be ready
To see dat ship sail by.

150   I'm a-Rolling

Traditional   Traditional

I'm a-roll - ing, I'm a-roll - ing, I'm a-roll-ing thro' an un-friend-ly world;

I'm a-roll - ing, I'm a - roll - ing thro' an un - friend-ly world.

Verses
Unison

1. O broth-ers, won't you help me, O broth-ers, won't you help me to pray?
2. O sis - ters, won't you help me, O sis - ters, won't you help me to pray?
3. O preach-ers, won't you help me, O preach-ers, won't you help me to pray?

O broth-ers, won't you help me, Won't you help me in the ser-vice of the Lord?_
O sis - ters, won't you help me, Won't you help me in the ser-vice of the Lord?_
O preach-ers, won't you help me, Won't you help me in the ser-vice of the Lord?_

I Want to Be Ready

Traditional
Harm. by J. Jefferson Cleveland, 1937-
and Verolga Nix, 1933-

151

Traditional

Lively
Refrain

I want to be read - y, I want to be read - y,___

Fine

I want to be read - y to walk in Je - ru - sa - lem just like John.

Leader

Response

1. O John, O John, what do you say?
2. John said the cit - y was just four-square Walk in Je-ru-sa-lem just like John.
3. When Pe-ter was preach-ing at Pen - te - cost,

Leader

Response

D.C.

That I'll be there at the com-ing day,
And he de - clared he'd meet me there, Walk in Je-ru-sa-lem just like John.
He was en- dowed with the Ho- ly Ghost,

152   King Jesus Is a-Listenin'

Traditional

Traditional   Arr. by J. Jefferson Cleveland, 1937-

Refrain Spirited

Leader   **Response**   **Leader**   **Response**

King Je-sus is a-lis-ten-in' all day long, King Je-sus is a-lis-ten-in' all day

Leader   **Response**   *Fine*

long, King Je-sus is a-lis-ten-in' all day long, To hear some sin-ner pray.

Verses

1. Some say that John the Bap-tist Was noth-in' but a Jew,
2. That Gos-pel train is com-in', A-rum-blin' through the lan',
3. I know I been con-vert-ed, I ain't gon' make no a-larm,

rit.   *D.C. al Fine*

But the Ho-ly Bi-ble tells us That John was a preach-er too.
But I hear them wheels a-hum-min', Get read-y to board that train!
For my soul is bound for Glo-ry, And the dev-il can't do me no harm.

Oh, Mary, Don't You Weep, Don't You Mourn

Traditional   Traditional

154 Somebody's Knocking at Your Door

Traditional
Harm by J. Jefferson Cleveland, 1937-
and Verolga Nix, 1933-

Traditional

Some-bod-y's knock-ing at your door, Some-bod-y's knock-ing at your door,

O sin-ner, why don't you an-swer? Some-bod-y's knock-ing at your door.

1. Knocks like Je-sus, Some-bod-y's knock-ing at your door.

Knocks like Je-sus, Some-bod-y's knock-ing at your door.

2. **Leader:** Can't you hear Him?
    Response: Somebody's knocking at your door.

3. **Leader:** Answer Jesus.
    Response: Somebody's knocking . .

4. **Leader:** Jesus calls you.
    Response: Somebody's knocking . .

5. **Leader:** Can't you trust Him?
    Response: Somebody's knocking . .

Sometimes I Feel Like a Moanin' Dove

155

Traditional
Arr. by J. Jefferson Cleveland, 1937-
and Verolga Nix, 1933-

Traditional

Traditional   Traditional

Joyfully

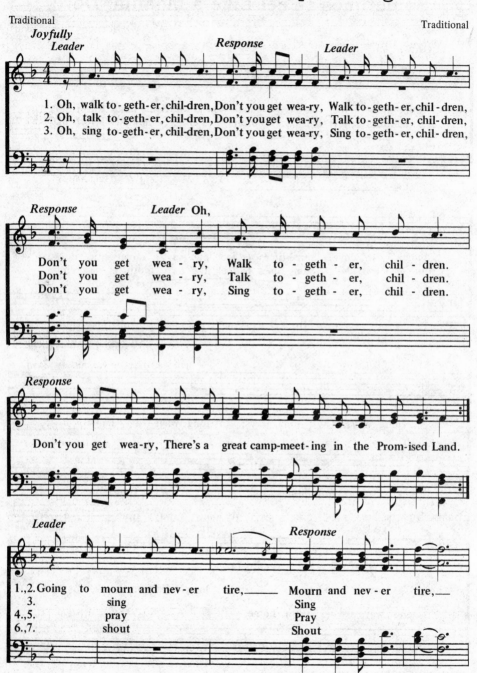

1. Oh, walk to-geth-er, chil-dren, Don't you get wea-ry, Walk to-geth-er, chil-dren,
2. Oh, talk to-geth-er, chil-dren, Don't you get wea-ry, Talk to-geth-er, chil-dren,
3. Oh, sing to-geth-er, chil-dren, Don't you get wea-ry, Sing to-geth-er, chil-dren,

Don't you get wea-ry, Walk to - geth - er, chil - dren.
Don't you get wea-ry, Talk to - geth - er, chil - dren.
Don't you get wea-ry, Sing to - geth - er, chil - dren.

Don't you get wea-ry, There's a great camp-meet-ing in the Prom-ised Land.

1.,2. Going to mourn and nev-er tire,___ Mourn and nev-er tire,___
3.   sing   Sing
4.,5.   pray   Pray
6.,7.   shout   Shout

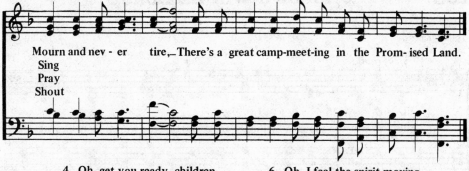

Mourn and nev - er tire,—There's a great camp-meet-ing in the Prom-ised Land.
Sing
Pray
Shout

4. Oh, get you ready, children, . . .   6. Oh, I feel the spirit moving, . . .
5. For Jesus is a - coming, . . .   7. Oh, now I'm getting happy, . . .

On Ma Journey   157

Traditional   Traditional

Refrain
Lively

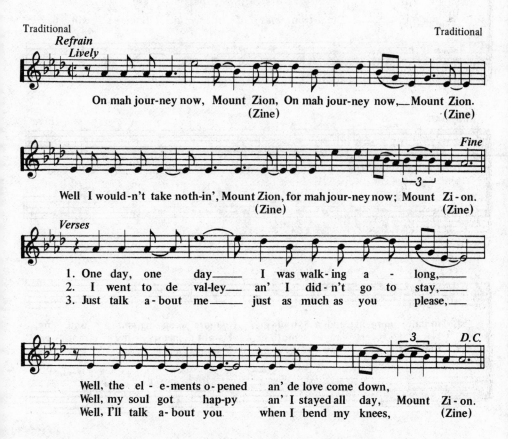

On mah jour-ney now, Mount Zion, On mah jour-ney now,—Mount Zion.
(Zine)   (Zine)

Fine

Well I would-n't take noth-in', Mount Zion, for mah jour-ney now; Mount Zi-on.
(Zine)   (Zine)

Verses

1. One day, one day___ I was walk-ing a - long,___
2. I went to de val-ley___ an' I did-n't go to stay,___
3. Just talk a - bout me___ just as much as you please,___

D.C.

Well, the el - e-ments o-pened an' de love come down,
Well, my soul got hap-py an' I stayed all day, Mount Zi-on.
Well, I'll talk a-bout you when I bend my knees, (Zine)

Soon-a Will Be Done

Traditional   Traditional

Very rhythmic

Soon-a will be done-a with the trou-bles of the world, Trou-bles of the

world,_____ The trou-bles of the world. Soon-a will be

done-a with the trou-bles of the world. Goin' home to live with God. *Fine*

Solo or Unison

1. No more weep-ing and a - wail-ing, No more weep-ing and a - wail-ing,
2. I want t' meet my moth-er, I want t' meet my moth-er,
3. I want t' meet my Je - sus, I want t' meet my Je - sus,

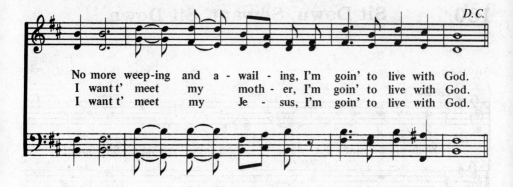

No more weep-ing and a - wail - ing, I'm goin' to live with God.
I want t' meet my moth - er, I'm goin' to live with God.
I want t' meet my Je - sus, I'm goin' to live with God.

Scandalize' My Name

159

Traditional

Traditional

Well, I met my 1. sis - ter
2. broth - er de oth - er day, Give him my___ right
3. preach - er

her
him
(her)

han', Jes' as soon as ev - er my back was turned he took 'n' scan-da-lize' my

she
he
(she)

name. Do you call dat a broth-er? No! No! you call dat a broth-er?
'li-gion? 'li-gion?

sis - ter? sis - ter?

No! No! you call dat a broth-er? No! No!___ scan-da-lize' my name.
'li-gion?

sis - ter?

160 Sit Down, Servant, Sit Down

Traditional

Traditional
Harm. by Verolga Nix, 1933-

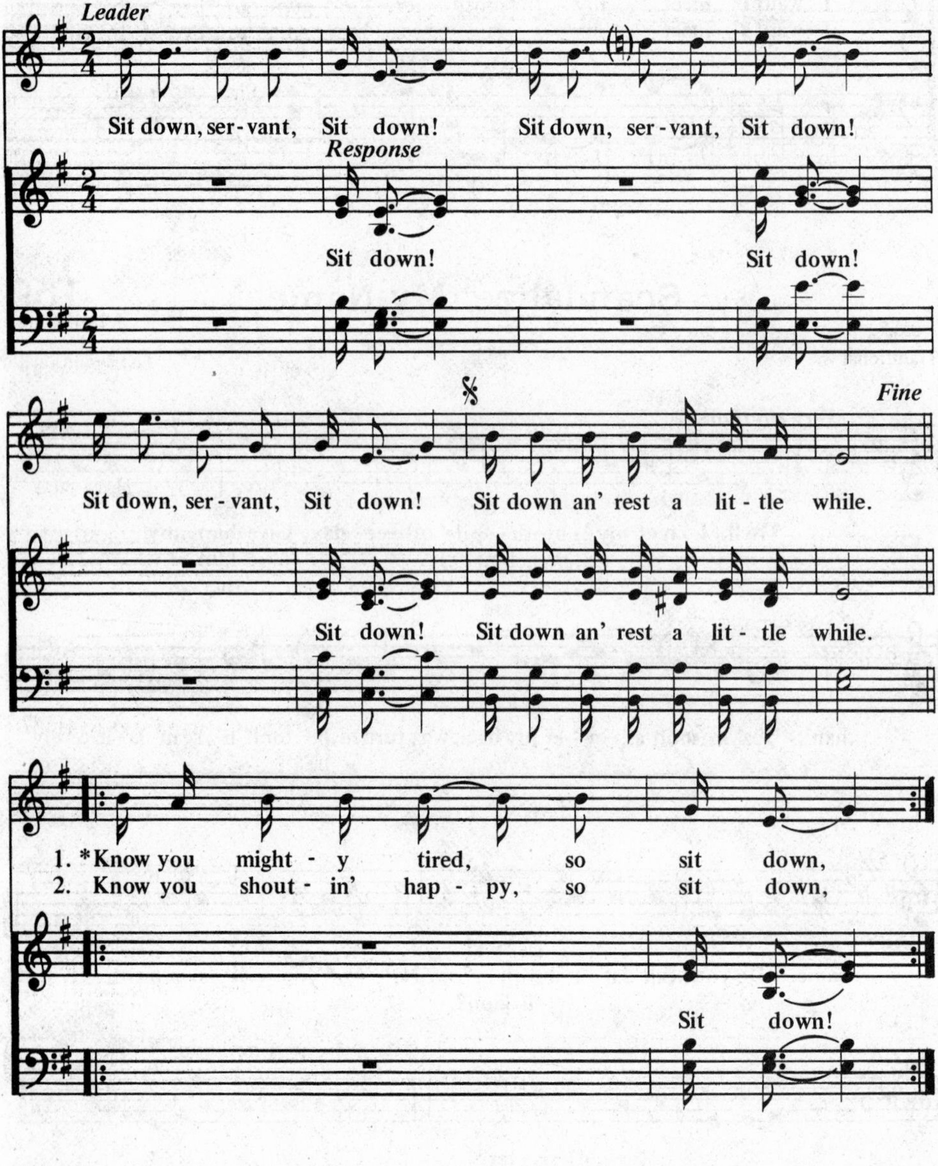
Leader
Sit down, ser - vant, Sit down! Sit down, ser - vant, Sit down!
Response
Sit down! Sit down!
Sit down, ser - vant, Sit down! Sit down an' rest a lit - tle while.
Fine
Sit down! Sit down an' rest a lit - tle while.
1. *Know you might - y tired, so sit down,
2. Know you shout - in' hap - py, so sit down,
Sit down!

*I know

know you might - y tired, so sit down!
know you shout - in' hap - py, so sit down!

Sit down!

Certainly, Lord

161

Traditional

Traditional

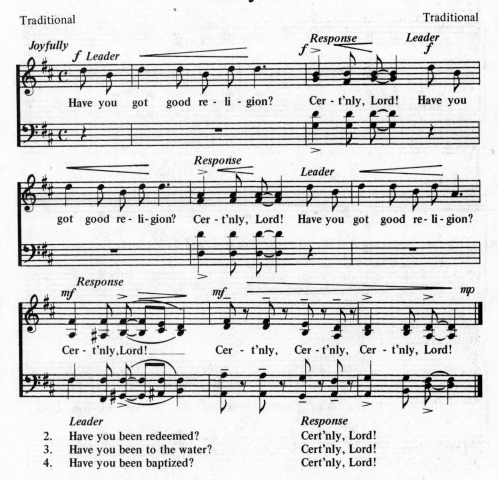

Joyfully

f Leader *Response* *Leader f*

Have you got good re - li - gion? Cer - t'nly, Lord! Have you

Response *Leader*

got good re - li - gion? Cer - t'nly, Lord! Have you got good re - li - gion?

Response

mf *mf* *mp*

Cer - t'nly, Lord! Cer - t'nly, Cer - t'nly, Cer - t'nly, Lord!

Leader	Response
2. Have you been redeemed?	Cert'nly, Lord!
3. Have you been to the water?	Cert'nly, Lord!
4. Have you been baptized?	Cert'nly, Lord!

Mary and Martha

Traditional   Traditional

1. Ma-ry and-a Mar-tha's just gone 'long, Ma-ry and-a Mar-tha's just gone 'long,

Ma - ry and - a Mar-tha's just gone 'long, To ring those charm-ing bells.

Refrain

Cry-ing free grace and dy-ing love, Free grace and dy-ing love, Free grace and

dy-ing love, To ring those charm-ing bells. Oh! way o - ver Jor-dan, Lord,

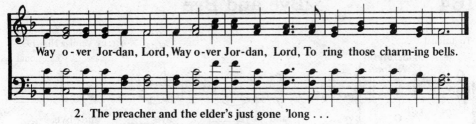

Way o-ver Jor-dan, Lord, Way o-ver Jor-dan, Lord, To ring those charm-ing bells.

2. The preacher and the elder's just gone 'long . . .
3. My father and mother's just gone 'long . . .
4. The Methodists and Baptists' just gone 'long . . .

My Good Lord's Done Been Here   163

Traditional

Traditional
Harm. by Verolga Nix. 1933-

Refrain
Lively

Oh, my Good Lord's done been here! Blessed my soul and gone a - way,

Fine

My Good Lord's done been here, Blessed my soul and gone.

Verses

1. When I get up in Heav - en   And - a my work is done, Goin' to
2. Hold up the Bap - tist fin - ger,   Hold up the Bap - tist hand,
3. You may be a white man,   White as the drift-ing snow, If your

D.S.

sit down by Sis - ter Ma - ry,   And chat-ter with the dar - lin' Son.
When I get in the Heav - ens,   Go-ing a - join the Bap - tist Band.
soul ain't been con - vert-ed,   To Hell you're sure to go.

164

Bye and Bye

Traditional

Traditional
Arr. by Verolga Nix, 1933-

O bye— and bye,— bye— and bye,

O bye and bye, yes, bye and bye

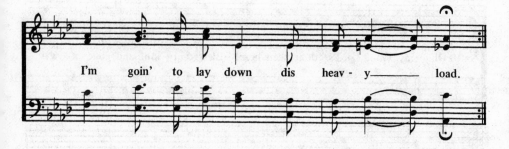

I'm goin' to lay down dis heav - y— load.

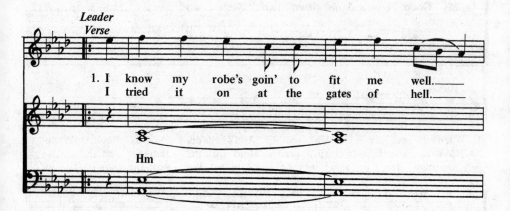

Leader
Verse

1. I know my robe's goin' to fit me well.—
I tried it on at the gates of hell.—

Hm

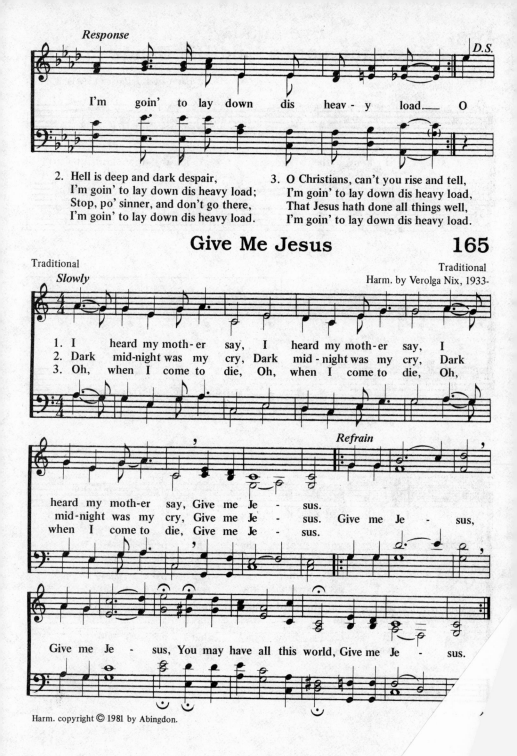

Response

D.S.

I'm goin' to lay down dis heav-y load.— O

2. Hell is deep and dark despair,
   I'm goin' to lay down dis heavy load;
   Stop, po' sinner, and don't go there,
   I'm goin' to lay down dis heavy load.

3. O Christians, can't you rise and tell,
   I'm goin' to lay down dis heavy load,
   That Jesus hath done all things well,
   I'm goin' to lay down dis heavy load.

Give Me Jesus

165

Traditional

Traditional
Harm. by Verolga Nix, 1933-

Slowly

1. I heard my moth-er say, I heard my moth-er say, I
2. Dark mid-night was my cry, Dark mid-night was my cry, Dark
3. Oh, when I come to die, Oh, when I come to die, Oh,

heard my moth-er say, Give me Je - sus.
mid-night was my cry, Give me Je - sus. Give me Je - sus,
when I come to die, Give me Je - sus.

Refrain

Give me Je - sus, You may have all this world, Give me Je - sus.

Harm. copyright © 1981 by Abingdon.

I Know the Lord's Laid His Hands on Me

Traditional

Traditional
Harm. by J. Jefferson Cleveland, 1937-

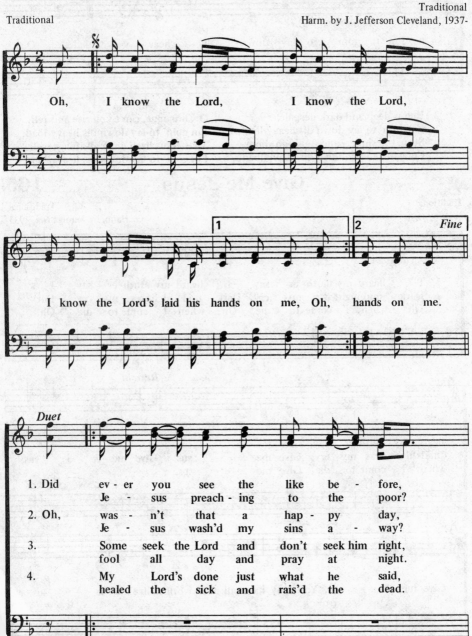

Oh, I know the Lord, I know the Lord,

I know the Lord's laid his hands on me, Oh, hands on me.

Duet

1. Did	ev - er	you	see	the	like be -	fore,
	Je -	sus	preach - ing	to	the	poor?
2. Oh,	was -	n't	that	a	hap - py	day,
	Je -	sus	wash'd	my	sins a -	way?
3.	Some	seek the Lord	and	don't	seek him	right,
	fool	all	day	and	pray	at	night.
4.	My	Lord's	done	just	what	he	said,
	healed	the	sick	and	rais'd	the	dead.

Response

| 1 | | 2 | D.S. |

I know the Lord's laid his hands on me, King hands on me. Oh,
I know the Lord's laid his

I know the Lord's laid his hands on me, When hands on me. Oh,
I know the Lord's laid his

I know the Lord's laid his hands on me, They hands on me. Oh,
I know the Lord's laid his

I know the Lord's laid his hands on me, He's hands on me. Oh,
I know the Lord's laid his

Over My Head   **167**

Traditional
Arr. by J. Jefferson Cleveland, 1937-
and Verolga Nix, 1933-

Traditional

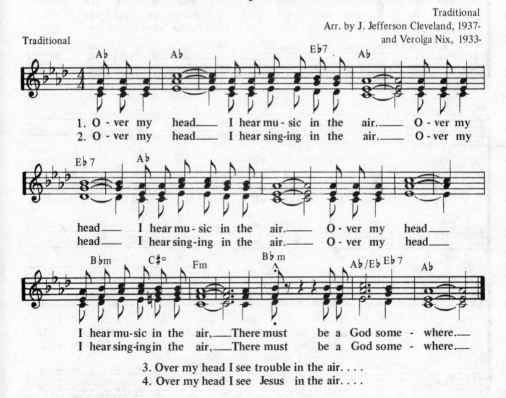

1. O - ver my head__ I hear mu - sic in the air.__ O - ver my
2. O - ver my head__ I hear sing-ing in the air.__ O - ver my

head__ I hear mu - sic in the air.__ O - ver my head__
head__ I hear sing-ing in the air.__ O - ver my head__

I hear mu-sic in the air,__There must be a God some - where.__
I hear sing-ing in the air,__There must be a God some - where.__

3. Over my head I see trouble in the air. . . .
4. Over my head I see Jesus in the air. . . .

168 He Arose

Traditional

Traditional

1. They cru - ci - fied my Sav - ior and nailed Him to the cross,
2. And Jo - seph begged His bod - y and laid it in the tomb,
3. Sister Ma - ry, she came run - ning, a - look - ing for my Lord,
4. An an - gel came from heav - en and rolled the stone a - way,

They cru - ci - fied my Sav - ior and nailed Him to the cross,
And Jo - seph begged His bod - y and laid it in the tomb,
Sister Ma - ry, she came run - ning, a - look - ing for my Lord,
An an - gel came from heav - en and rolled the stone a - way,

cross, And the Lord will bear my spir - it home.
tomb, And the Lord will bear my spir - it home.
Lord, And the Lord will bear my spir - it home.
way, And the Lord will bear my spir - it home.

He 'rose, He 'rose, He 'rose from the dead, He 'rose, He 'rose, He
He 'rose, He 'rose, He 'rose, He 'rose,

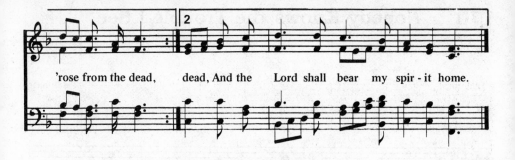

'rose from the dead, dead, And the Lord shall bear my spir - it home.

Oh! What a Beautiful City 169

Traditional

Traditional

Refrain

Oh! what a beau - ti - ful cit - y, Oh! what a beau - ti - ful cit - y,

Oh! what a beau - ti - ful cit - y, Twelve gates - a to the cit - y, Hal - le - lu!

Verses

1. Three gates in - a de east, Three gates in - a de west,
2. My Lord built - a dat city, Said it was just - a fo' square;

Three gates in - a de north, And three gates in - a de south,
Want - ed all - a you sinners To meet Him in - a de air;

Mak - ing it twelve gates - a to de cit - y - a, Hal - le - lu!
'cause He built twelve gates - a to de cit - y - a, Hal - le - lu!

170 Nobody Knows the Trouble I See

Traditional   Traditional

Refrain

No-bod-y knows the trou-ble I see, No-bod-y knows my sor-row;

Fine

No-bod-y knows the trou-ble I see, Glo-ry, hal-le-lu-jah!

Duet or other voices

All

1. Some-times I'm up, some-times I'm down, Oh, yes, Lord!
2. Al-though you see me going 'long so, Oh, yes, Lord!
3. What makes old Sa-tan hate me so? Oh, yes, Lord!

Duet or other voices

All　　　　　　　　*D.C. al Fine*

Some -	times	I'm	al -	most	to	the	groun',	Oh,	yes,	Lord!
I	have	my	trou -	bles	here	be -	low,	Oh,	yes,	Lord!
'Cause	he	got	me	once	and	let	me	go,	Oh,	yes,	Lord!

171
Nobody Knows the Trouble I See, Lord!

Traditional　　　　　　　　　　　　　　　　Traditional

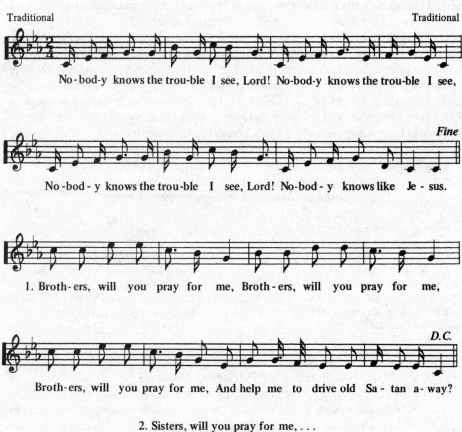

No-bod-y knows the trou-ble I see, Lord! No-bod-y knows the trou-ble I see,

Fine

No-bod-y knows the trou-ble I see, Lord! No-bod-y knows like Je - sus.

1. Broth-ers, will you pray for me, Broth-ers, will you pray for me,

D.C.

Broth-ers, will you pray for me, And help me to drive old Sa - tan a-way?

2. Sisters, will you pray for me, . . .
3. Mothers, will you pray for me, . . .
4. Preachers, will you pray for me, . . .

A Historical Account of the Black Gospel Song

Generally, the gospel-song phenomenon in America came into existence during the latter part of the nineteenth century and, from its inception, was connected with congregational singing. The name "gospel" was assigned to these songs because many of the texts were derived from the first four books of the New Testament. Also many of the texts dealt with the teachings of Jesus and of the Christian church; many of the texts were closely connected with the doctrine of salvation by grace. It became a part of the regular services of the church and addressed itself, more often than not, to common life experiences. More specifically, gospel music, as it is related to the Black experience, is an indigenous product of the Black church, having first become popular in the early 1920s (this genre of music is most popular among the poor Blacks, though in recent years—within the last fifteen—middle class and wealthy Blacks have exalted its virtues more and more). In contrast to the Black "spiritual," whose inception was in the cotton fields and in the rural setting of the camp meeting where large numbers of Blacks gathered in the open to listen to itinerant preachers, the gospel song came about in urban settings. Huge temporary tents erected for revival meetings by touring evangelists, as well as large tabernacles, were the settings where the early gospel music flourished. Eileen Southern states:

> When the Black people began pouring into the nation's cities during the second decade of the twentieth century, they took their joyful spirituals with them, but found the rural born music to be unsatisfactory in urban settings and unresponsive to their needs. Consequently the church singers created a more expressive music to which they applied the term gospel, but which displayed little resemblance to the traditional gospel songs of the Whites. Negro gospel music became essentially the sacred counterpart of the city blues, sung in the same improvisatory tradition with piano, guitar, or instrumental accompaniment.[1]

Therefore, we readily detect a direct historical, religious, and musical lineage between the Black gospel and other indigenous music genres.

The popularity of gospel music among Blacks increased after its inception in the Black church, but this popularity existed in the ghettos and its store-front churches since the ultra-sophisticated larger Baptist and Methodist churches did not

---

1. Eileen Southern, *The Music of Black Americans* (New York: W. W. Norton, 1971), p. 402.

readily accept this music genre in the beginning—mainly because of its similarities to the "mundane" blues.

Gradually, the popularity of Black gospel spread from the church, and individual performers and writers of vaudeville and blues began to switch to gospel performing and writing. Thomas A. Dorsey (1899–   ) is by far the most famous of this group. He is commonly known as the originator of the Black gospel style; he bestows this honor, in turn, without reservation upon the late Dr. Charles A. Tindley (1865–1933). In 1921 at the National Baptist Convention held at Dorsey's Pilgrim Baptist Church in Chicago, he heard the late A. W. Nix sing "I Do, Don't You?"[2] and was so impressed with the song that he decided to write church music that would move others the way he had been moved. His first gospel songs were typical revival and tabernacle songs in the style of Tindley, to whom he felt indebted for changing his musical emphasis and interest from blues to religious music. More than anyone else, Tindley was Dorsey's idol.

Dorsey began to compose gospel songs while still performing occasionally in the blues and vaudeville circuits. His first gospel hit, "If You See My Saviour, Tell Him That You Saw Me," was composed in 1926. Dorsey, like Tindley, was influenced by the old hymns of Dr. Watts, and Dorsey's version of "The Day Is Past and Gone" became one of his most popular songs. Others followed shortly, including "It's My Desire" and "When I've Done the Best I Can." In 1932, Dorsey's first wife and his only child died while he was touring. A week later, he had composed his masterpiece, "Precious Lord, Take My Hand," a song that combines *intense religious devotion* and *reaction to realism,* and that remains the most popular of his more than four hundred songs.

> Precious Lord, take my hand,
> Lead me on, let me stand,
> I am tired, I am weak, I am worn.
> Through the storm, through the night,
> Lead me on to the Light,
> Take my hand, precious Lord, lead me on.

Wyatt Tee Walker suggests a division of gospel music into two categories, *historical* and *modern.*

The gospel music that was born with Dorsey as its chief architect is considered . . . *HISTORIC GOSPEL.* . . . That music was penned by Dorsey, Kenneth Morris, Theodore Frye, Doris Akers, Roberta Martin, Lucie Campbell, W. H. Brewster, Sr., and others. . . . *MODERN GOSPEL* is a fairly recent phenomenon; it begins with the tail end of the quartet era in the fifties and the radical social change that developed in the early sixties. Its presence and form are still evolving. Modern Gospel. . . . reflects the influences of both the quartet era and the period symbolized by Martin Luther King's leadership. . . . The appearance of Modern Gospel did not in any way mark the demise of

---

2. "I Do, Don't You?" has been erroneously attributed to Charles Tindley. It was in fact, composed by a White man whose name was E. O. Excell (1851–1921). Tindley was given the credit because Excell composed the song in the hymn style of Tindley.

Historic Gospel. Both are very much in evidence, and they exist in parallel fashion with little or no problem.[3]

During the fifties and sixties, many professional gospel groups emerged and began touring the country—singing in small churches, auditoriums, tabernacles, and concert halls. Some of the most famous were the Sallie Martin Singers, and the Roberta Martin Singers, the Ward Singers (featuring Clara Ward and Marion Williams), the Davis Sisters, the Caravans (featuring Shirley Caesar), the Gospel Harmonettes (featuring Dorothy Love Coates), the Dixie Humming Birds, the Soul Stirrers (featuring Sam Cooke), the Staple Singers, and the Alex Bradford Singers.

Many of these groups produced lead singers who later became renowned in blues and popular music. Sam Cooke of the Soul Stirrers, Dinah Washington of the Sallie Martin Singers, Dionne Warwick of the Drinkard Singers, Marie Knight of the Marie Knight–Rosetta Thorpe Duo, and Thelma Houston of the Art Reynolds Singers are examples. (The famous Original Five Blind Boys were an early influence on Ray Charles.) Among those solo gospel performers who remained faithful to the genre were the late Mahalia Jackson, the late Brother Joe May, Shirley Caesar, Marion Williams, Cassietta George, James Cleveland, and Dorothy Love Coates. Of course, there were those who began as gospel solo performers and later switched to other genres. The most renowned personality among this group is the extremely talented Aretha Franklin, who began singing as a very young child in her father's church in Detroit, Michigan—the New Bethel Baptist Church. The Reverend C. L. Franklin, her father, achieved somewhat limited renown himself as a gospel singer.

The emphasis in the 1970s on Black awareness and all its emotionalism has resulted in a renewed popularity of gospel music. This is due in large part to the emotional nature of the music. It has been said that there is hardly an emotion that gospel music cannot stir. It seems that more than older generations, the Black youth in the church, in the colleges, and in the community are recapturing the meaning of and revitalizing the Black gospel as part of their concern for Black awareness. Prestigious Black academic institutions, such as Fisk Universty in Nashville, Tennessee, and Howard University in Washington, D.C., which were White-oriented until a few years ago, have had to answer their students' demands for Black gospel choirs as part of their campus activities. Even predominantly White schools, with representative numbers of Black students have had to acquiesce. Almost every Black church nowadays has at least one gospel choir made up mostly of young people, and they are excellent groups. On the other hand, many young Blacks are leaving churches where there is a paucity of Black music or where this music has to take a back seat to the European-style religious music. Others have formed community gospel choirs, many interdenominational. The Baptist, Catholic, and Methodist (B C and M) Gospel Choir of Nashville, Tennessee, is a prime example.

Numerous excellent soloists, ensembles, and choirs have developed during this new emphasis on gospel music. They are exponents of what is now called

---

3. Wyatt Tee Walker, *Somebody's Calling My Name* (Valley Forge, Pa.: Judson Press, 1979), pp. 127-31.

contemporary or rock gospel, and some of the most talented musicians in the world are to be found among them: Edwin Hawkins and his Singers, Walter Hawkins and the Love Center Choir, the New York Community Gospel Choir, the Southern California Community Choir, Andrae Crouch and the Disciples, Dannibelle, Sara Jordan Powell, Jessye Dixon, Shirley Caesar, and Billy Preston. Black gospel will be around for many years to come, and its popularity has been greatly enhanced by the recording industry. It is now included in approximately 95 percent of all the Black churches in this country. As with other types of music, the mass media and business interests have caused gospel music to become commercial. It has made its way into the night clubs of Las Vegas; it can be found at the Newport Jazz Festival; New York's Philharmonic Hall in Lincoln Center for the Performing Arts has welcomed it; Symphony Hall at Boston has promoted it; the Academy of Music in Philadelphia has opened its doors to it; London, Paris, Munich, Berlin—all have received it with open arms, and royalty around the world command performances.

Tony Heilbut states that "Gospel is more than music: it is one of the central experiences of Black America, a common heritage whose vitality was a means of survival in a hostile world."[4] The Black church is among the most vital institutions to Blacks in this country, and Black gospel *is* an important phase of that experience. It is a part of the Black heritage, therefore, its history must be taught, preserved, and respected.

J. Jefferson Cleveland

---

4. Tony Heilbut, *The Gospel Sound*, New York: Simon and Schuster, 1971).

173 Lord, Don't Move This Mountain

Doris Akers

Mahalia Jackson, 1911-1972

Refrain

Lord, don't move the moun - tain,＿ but give me strength to climb it. Please don't move ＿ that stum - bl - ing block, ＿ But

lead me, Lord,— a- round it. 1. The round it.
2. Now
3. Our

way may not— be eas - y._____ You
when my foes— would slay me._____ And
cares we bring— un - to you._____ You

did - n't say that it would be. For
these things they will try to do. Oh,
told us that— we— could. For

when my trib-u-la-tions get___ too light____ I
Lord, don't touch them, but with-in___ their hearts,____ make
you help those who try to help___ them-selves____ and

tend to stray___ from___ Thee.
them give their___ hearts to you;
I be-lieve___ we___ should.

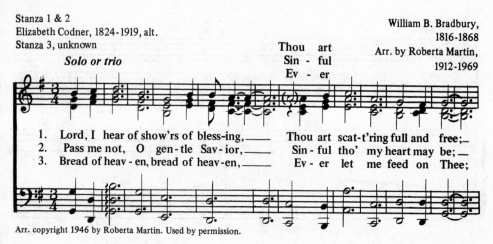

174

Even Me

Stanza 1 & 2
Elizabeth Codner, 1824-1919, alt.
Stanza 3, unknown

William B. Bradbury,
1816-1868
Arr. by Roberta Martin,
1912-1969

Solo or trio

Thou art
Sin - ful
Ev - er

1. Lord, I hear of show'rs of bless-ing,___ Thou art scat-t'ring full and free;___
2. Pass me not, O gen-tle Sav-ior,___ Sin-ful tho' my heart may be;___
3. Bread of heav-en, bread of heav-en,___ Ev-er let me feed on Thee;

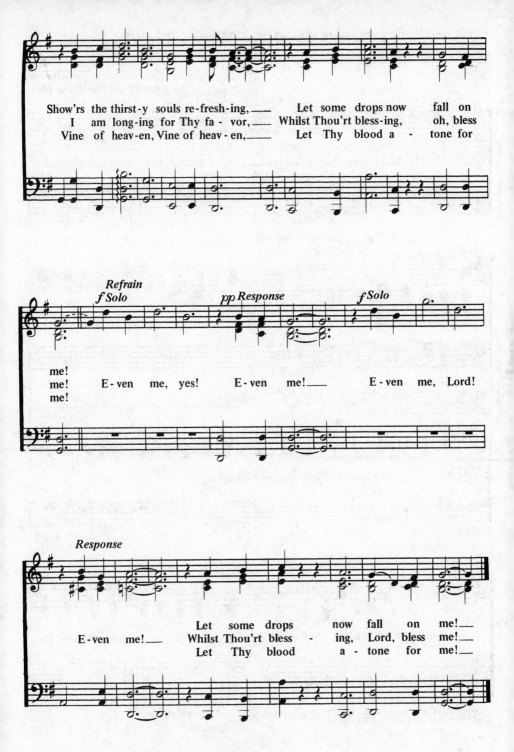

Show'rs the thirst-y souls re-fresh-ing, ___ Let some drops now fall on
I am long-ing for Thy fa - vor, ___ Whilst Thou'rt bless-ing, oh, bless
Vine of heav-en, Vine of heav - en, ___ Let Thy blood a - tone for

Refrain
f Solo   *pp* Response   *f* Solo

me!
me!   E-ven me, yes!   E-ven me! ___   E-ven me, Lord!
me!

Response

                Let some drops   now fall on me! ___
E-ven me! ___   Whilst Thou'rt bless - ing, Lord, bless me! ___
                Let Thy blood a - tone for me! ___

175 I Don't Feel No Ways Tired

Curtis Burrell
Arr. by Kenneth Morris, 1916-

C. B.

I don't feel no ways tired,___ I come too far from where I start - ed from,___ No - bod - y told me that the road would be eas - y,___ I don't be - lieve He brought me this far to leave me.___

1. brought me this far, I don't be - lieve He brought me this far, I don't be - lieve He

Keep repeating until ready to go on

I Don't Care What the World May Do 176

A. B.

Alex Bradford, d. 1978
Arr. by Roberta Martin, 1912-1969

Copyright 1953 by Roberta Martin. International copyright secured.

let His prais-es ring ev-ery day,____ Walk-ing

Going to let His prais-es ring ev-ery day, Walk-ing

by my side my ev-ery step He'll guide,____ I don't

by my side my ev-ery step He'll guide,____

care what the world may do, I'm going to praise His name.

I don't care what the world may do, I'm going to praise His name.

Verses

1. Ev - ery day while walk - ing a - long I know I'm in His care___ I know
2. Trou - ble I don't mind no more, since I'm in the fold___ I know

1. Ev - ery day while walk - ing a - long I know I'm in His care___
2. Trou - ble I don't mind no more, since I'm in the fold___

Je - sus is talk - ing with me While my friends and
Sa - tan can't harm me now Be - cause God

Je - sus is talk - ing with me While my friends and
Sa - tan can't harm me now Be - cause God

en - e - mies stare. How can I be an - gry when my
has con - trol. As I walk through the shadow of death

en - e - mies stare. How can I be an - gry when
has con - trol. As I walk through the shadow of death

God___ a - bides with - in? So__ I, I,
There'll be my God Him - self. So__ I won't

my God a - bides with - in? I, I,
There'll be my God Him - self. I won't

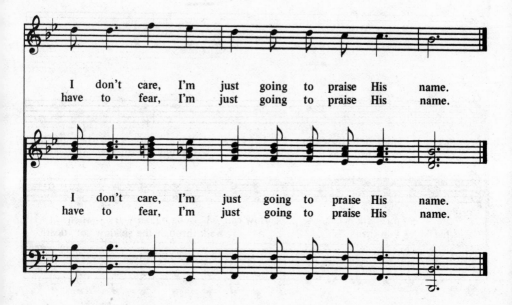

I don't care, I'm just going to praise His name.
have to fear, I'm just going to praise His name.

I don't care, I'm just going to praise His name.
have to fear, I'm just going to praise His name.

Until I Found the Lord

C. W.

Clara Ward
Arr. by Dorothy Pearson

1. Lord, I cried, I cried, I
2. Lord, I moaned, I moaned, I
3. Lord, I prayed, I prayed, I

I cried, yes, I cried, I cried all night long,
I moaned, yes, I moaned, I moaned all night long,
I prayed, yes, I prayed, I prayed all night long,

cried,
moaned,
prayed,

Un-til I found the Lord, My soul

I cried, yes, I cried un-til I found the Lord.
I moaned, yes, I moaned un-til I found the Lord.
I prayed, yes, I prayed un-til I found the Lord.

Oh, my soul, Oh, my soul.

Just could-n't rest con-tent-ed, just could-n't rest con-tent-ed,

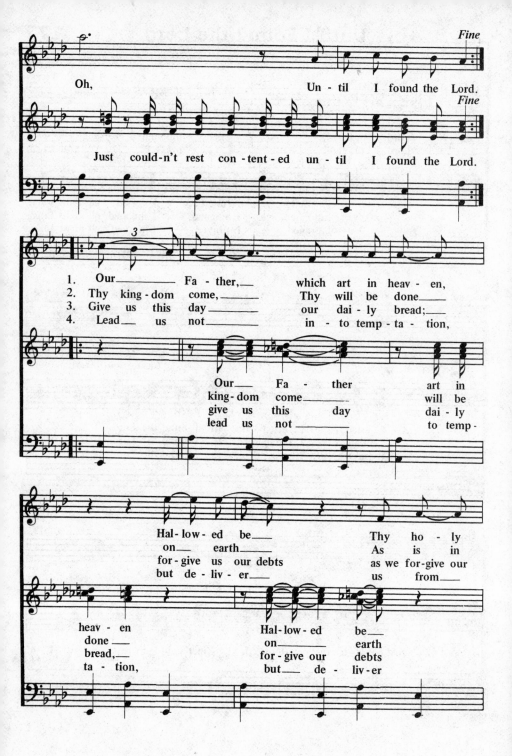

Fine

Oh,   Un - til   I found the   Lord.

Fine

Just   could-n't rest con -tent-ed un - til   I found the Lord.

1. Our_____ Fa - ther,___ which art in heav - en,
2. Thy king - dom come,_____ Thy will be done___
3. Give us this day_____ our dai - ly bread;___
4. Lead_ us not_____ in - to temp - ta - tion,

Our_ Fa - ther   art in
king - dom come_____ will be
give us this day   dai - ly
lead us not_____ to temp -

Hal - low - ed be_ Thy ho - ly
on_ earth_ As is in
for - give us our debts as we for-give our
but de - liv - er_ us from_

heav - en Hal - low - ed be_
done_ on_____ earth
bread,_ for - give our debts
ta - tion, but_ de - liv - er

178
He Understands, He'll Say "Well Done"

L. E. C.

Lucie E. Campbell

1. If when you give the best of your ser-vice, Tell-ing the world
2. Mis-un-der-stood, the Sav-ior of sin-ners, Hung on the cross;
3. If when this life of la-bor is end-ed, And the re-ward
4. But if you try and fail in your try-ing, Hands sore and scarred

that the Sav-ior is come; Be not dis-mayed when men don't be-
He was God's on-ly Son; Oh! hear Him call-ing His Fa-ther
of the race you have run; Oh! the sweet rest pre-pared for the
from the work you've be-gun; Take up your cross, run quick-ly to

lieve you; He un-der-stands; He'll say, "Well done."
in Heav'n, "Not my will, but Thine be done."
faith-ful Will be His blest and fi-nal "Well done."
meet Him; He'll un-der-stand, He'll say, "Well done."

Refrain

Oh, when I come to the end of my jour-ney, Wea-ry of life and the bat-tle is won; Car-r'ing the staff and cross of re-demp-tion, He'll un-der-stand, and say "Well done."

179   Precious Lord, Take My Hand

T. A. D.

Thomas A. Dorsey, 1899-

Pre-cious Lord, take my hand, Lead me on, let me stand, I am tired, I am weak, I am worn; Thru the storm, thru the night, Lead me on to the light, Take my hand, pre-cious Lord, Lead me home.

Verses

1. When my way grows drear, pre-cious Lord, lin-ger near, When my
2. When the dark-ness ap-pears and the night draws near, And the

life is al-most gone, Hear my cry, hear my call, Hold my
day is past and gone, At the riv-er I stand, Guide my

hand lest I fall; Take my hand, pre-cious Lord, Lead me home.
feet, hold my hand; Take my hand, pre-cious Lord, Lead me home.

180 Christ Is All

K.M.

Kenneth Morris, 1916-

Slow, with feeling
Verses

1. I don't pos - sess hous - es or lands, fine clothes or jewel-ry,_____
2. There are some folk who look and long for this world's rich-es,_____
3. Yes, Christ is all, means more to me than this world's rich-es,_____

Sor - rows and cares in this old world my lot seems to be,_____
There are some folk who look for pow'r, pos - i - tion too,_____
He is my sight, my guid-ing light__ thru path - less seas,_____

But I have a Christ who paid the price way back on Cal - v'ry__
But I have a Christ all in my life, this makes me hap - py__
Yes, it's might -y nice to own a Christ who will my friend be__

And Christ is all, all and all this world to me._____
For Christ is all, all and all this world to me._____
Yes Christ is all, all and all this world to me. _____

181 Goin' Up Yonder

W. H.

Walter Hawkins

1. If you wan-na know where I'm go-ing, Where I'm go-ing soon. If an-y-bod-y asks you where I'm go-ing Where I'm go-ing

2. I can take the pain, the heart-aches they bring, The com-fort's there in know-ing I'll soon be gone. As God gives me grace, I'll run this race, un-til I see my Sav-ior

face to face.____ soon.____ I'm

Refrain

go-in' up yon - der!____ I'm go-in' up yon - der!__

____ I'm go-in' up yon - der____ to be with my

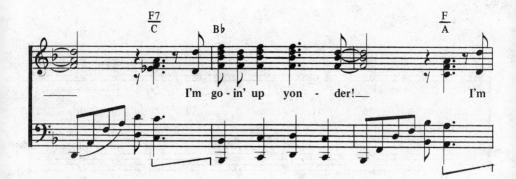

Give Me a Clean Heart

Margaret J. Douroux, 1941-
Arr. by Albert Denis Tessier

M. J. D.

Give me a clean heart so I may serve

Thee. Lord, fix my heart___ so that I___ may be used___ by

Thee. For I'm not wor - thy of all these bless -

ings. Give me a clean heart____ and I'll fol-low Thee.____

Verses

1. I'm not ask - ing for the rich - es of the land.____
   I am up and some-times I am down.____

I'm not ask - ing for high men to know my name.____
Some-times I am al - most lev - el to the ground.____

183 **I'll Fly Away**

Albert E. Brumley
Arr. by L. M. Bowles
and Theo R. Frye

A. E. B.

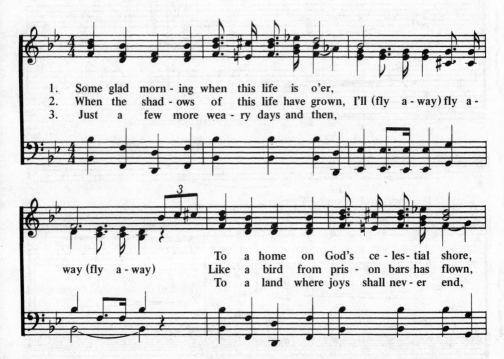

1. Some glad morn-ing when this life is o'er,
2. When the shad-ows of this life have grown, I'll (fly a-way) fly a-
3. Just a few more wea-ry days and then,

way (fly a-way)   To a home on God's ce-les-tial shore,
                  Like a bird from pris-on bars has flown,
                  To a land where joys shall nev-er end,

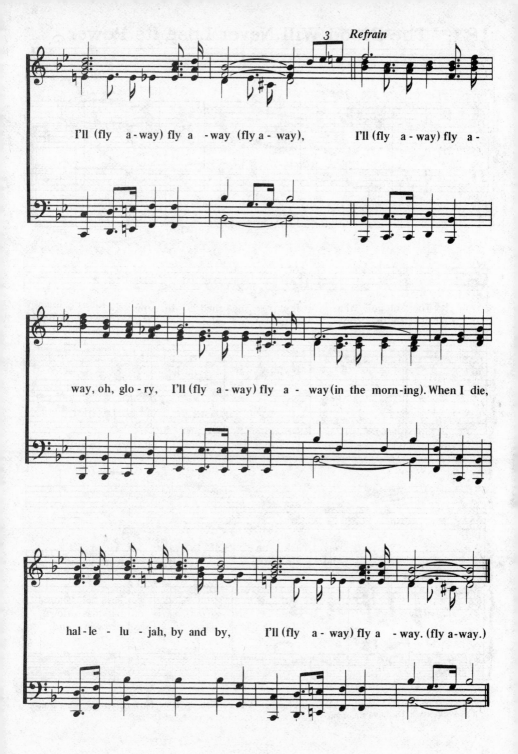

3 *Refrain*

I'll (fly a-way) fly a-way (fly a-way), I'll (fly a-way) fly a-way, oh, glo-ry, I'll (fly a-way) fly a-way (in the morn-ing). When I die, hal-le-lu-jah, by and by, I'll (fly a-way) fly a-way. (fly a-way.)

184 The Blood Will Never Lose Its Power

A.C.

Andrae Crouch, 1947-

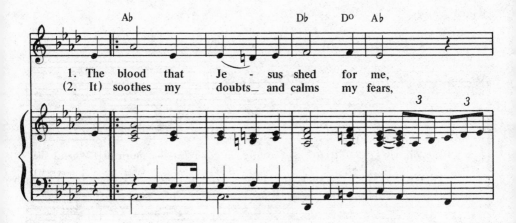

1. The blood that Je - sus shed for me,
(2. It) soothes my doubts_ and calms my fears,

Way back on Cal - va - ry, } The
And it dries all my tears, }

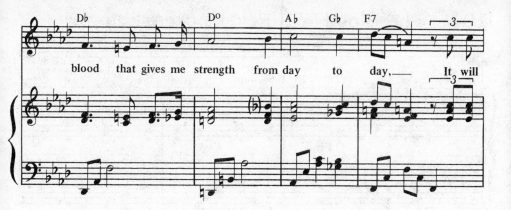

blood that gives me strength from day to day,___ It will

nev - er lose its pow'r.___

Refrain

It reach-es___ to the high - est moun - tain,___

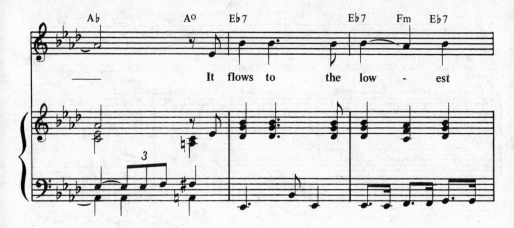

It flows to the low - est

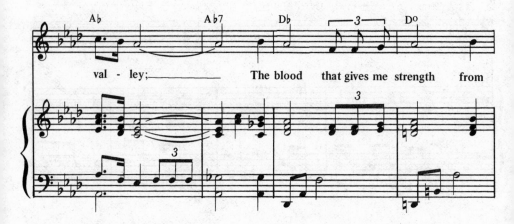

val - ley;_____ The blood that gives me strength from

day to day,_____ It will nev - er

185 Move Me

R. A. H.

Richard Alan Henderson, 1950-

Verse (Solo)

I want the Lord to move me,_____ so I can do His

will;_____ My emp-ty cup the Lord will fill.

I know He can, I know He will

Special Refrain *slightly faster*

186   If You Ask Him

Nezela W. Kirtz, 1939-

Richard Alan Henderson, 1950-

Solo

1. He'll lift you up__ if you ask Him, He'll show you the way.
2. He'll hold your hand_ if you ask Him, He'll give you strength a-new.
3. He'll com - fort you__ if you ask Him, He'll keep you thru the night.
4. He'll calm your fears_ if you ask Him, He'll give you peace of mind.

He'll fill your cup__ if you ask Him, He'll bright-en up your day._
He'll un - der - stand_ if you ask Him, He'll keep your' se - crets, too._
He'll stay__ with you if you ask Him, He'll make__ things all right._
He'll dry your tears __ if you ask Him, He'll give you joy di - vine_

see you thru,— see you thru,—

see you thru,— see you thru,— see you thru,—see you thru.—

187   Just to Behold His Face

Derricks Jackson
Arr. by Lucie E. Campbell

D. J.

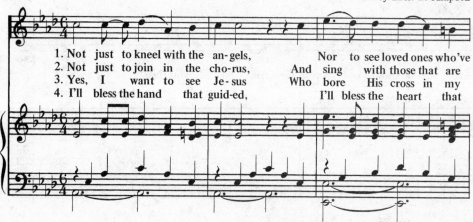

1. Not just to kneel with the an-gels,   Nor to see loved ones who've
2. Not just to join in the cho-rus,   And sing with those that are
3. Yes, I want to see Je-sus   Who bore His cross in my
4. I'll bless the hand that guid-ed,   I'll bless the heart that

gone, Not just to drink at the foun-tain
blest, And bathe my soul that is wea - ry,
stead; Who will - ing - ly suf - fered af - flic - tion
planned, I'll not rest un - til I see Je - sus

In the
With a
And He

Un - der the great white throne,
sea of heav - en - ly rest,
crown of thorns on His head;
takes me by the hand;

Not for the crown that He
But I'll look for the One who
Pre-cious Fount that was o-pened on
Fa - ther, moth - er and sis - ter and

giv - eth, That I'm try - ing to run this race;
saved me, From a death of sin and dis - grace;
Cal - v'ry, For me what a - maz - ing Grace,
broth er, And all who 'have won this race

'Twill be
What
Will be

All   I'll want up in heav-en,   Is   just   to be-hold His   face.
joy when I get up in heav-en,   Just   to   be-hold His   face.
joy will be mine there for-ev-er,   Just   to   be-hold His   face.
there   to join in that cho-rus,   As we all shall be-hold His   face.

Just   to be-hold His face,   Yes, just to be-hold His   face;

All   I will want up in heav-en,   Is just to be-hold His   face.

How I Got Over

Clara Ward, 1924-1973
Arr. by Dorothy Pearson

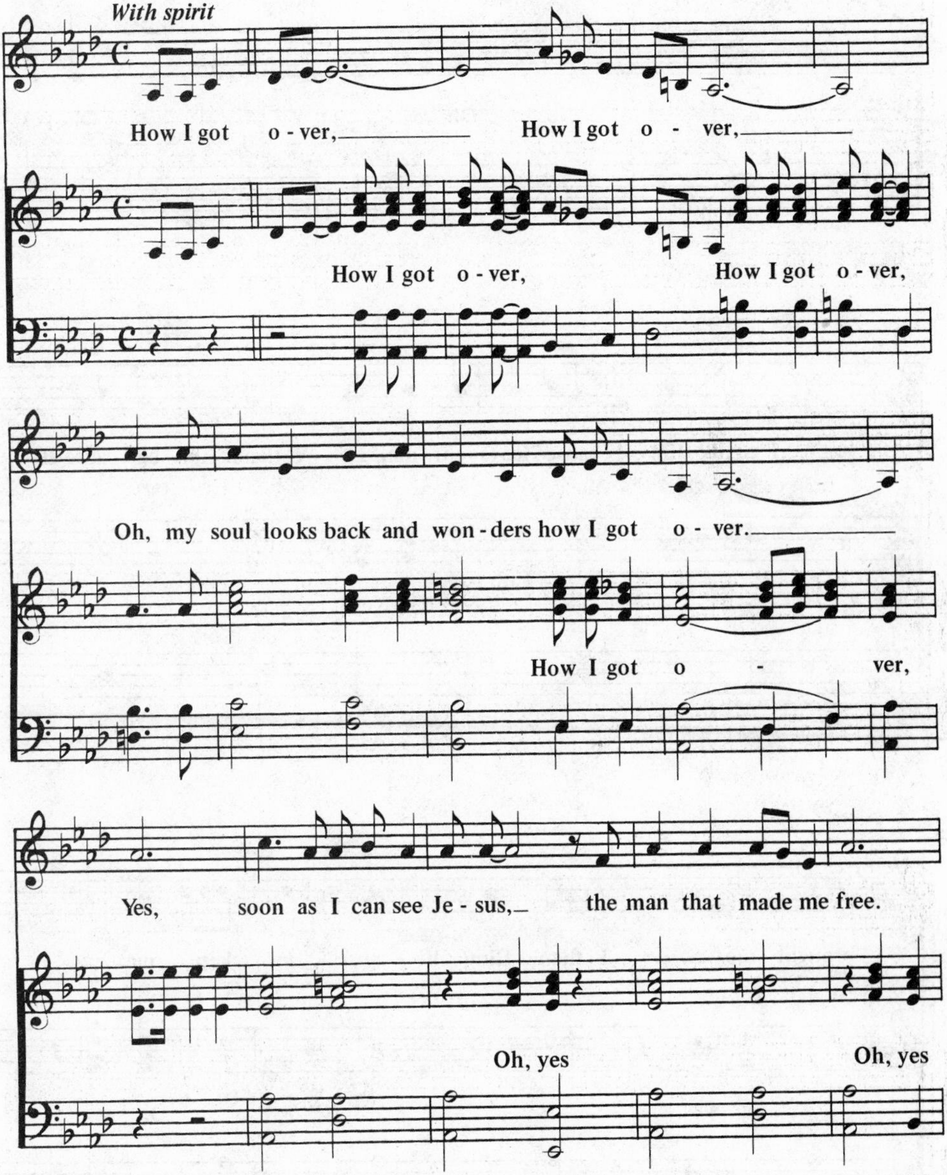

C. W.

With spirit

How I got o - ver,_____ How I got o - ver,_____

How I got o - ver, How I got o - ver,

Oh, my soul looks back and won - ders how I got o - ver._____

How I got o - ver,

Yes, soon as I can see Je - sus,___ the man that made me free.

Oh, yes Oh, yes

The man that bled and suf-fered and died for you and me.

Oh, yes Oh, yes

I thank Him be-cause He taught me.__ I thank Him be-cause He

Oh, yes

brought me.__ I thank Him be-cause He kept me.__

Oh, yes Oh, yes

189   Old Ship of Zion

T. A. D.

Thomas A. Dorsey, 1899-

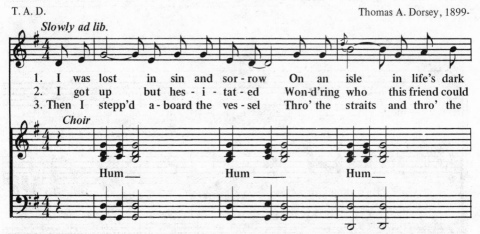

1. I was lost in sin and sor-row On an isle in life's dark
2. I got up but hes-i-tat-ed Won-d'ring who this friend could
3. Then I stepp'd a-board the ves-sel Thro' the straits and thro' the

Choir

Hum___   Hum____   Hum__

sea,   When I   saw   far in the dis-tance There a   ship   it seemed to
be,   Tho' the waves were wild and dash-ing   Seem-ing they would swal-low
gorge,   Man-y years it sail'd the wa-ters Man-y souls have made the

Hum___   Hum_   Hum____   Hum_

be,   Then I   saw   the cap-tain beck-on   Then he   called out loud and
me,   Then he raised his hand to-ward me Calm'd the wild and rag-ing
voyage, Then I rec-og-nized the cap-tain, It was Je-   sus in com-

Hum_   Hum___   Hum____   Hum_

free,   "I have come, my friend, to save you, Step on board and fol-low me."
sea,   With a voice so sweet and ten-der These words whis-per'd soft to me.
mand, 'Tis the old   ship of Zi-on And it's bound for Ca-naan land.

Hum___   Hum_   Hum____   Hum_   Hum_

Refrain

'Tis the old ship of Zi - on
There's no dan - ger in the wa - ter
She has land - ed man - y thou-sands,

'Tis the old
There's no dan - ger
She has land - ed

Old ship of Zi - on, old ship of Zi - on,
There's no dan - ger in the wa - ter,
She has land - ed man - y thou-sands

old ship of Zi - on, Oh, 'tis the old ship of
dan - ger in the wa - ter, Oh, there's no dan-ger in the
land - ed man - y thou-sands, Oh, she has land-ed man - y

old ship of Zi - on, Oh, yes, old ship of Zi - on,
there's no dan - ger, Oh, yes, there's no dan - ger
she has land-ed, Oh, yes, she has land-ed

Zi - on, Get on board, all of God's chil - dren, get on board.
wa - ter, Get on board, all of God's chil - dren, get on board.
thou-sands, Get on board, ear-ly one morn-ing, get on board.

old ship of Zi - on, all of God's chil - dren, get on board.
in the wa - ter, all of God's chil - dren, get on board.
man - y thou-sands, ear-ly one morn - ing, get on board.

For extra refrains: It will take you safely over, . . .
Do you think she'll make the journey, . . .
She's about to leave the landing, . . .

What Shall I Render?

Based on Ps. 116:12
M. P. D.

Margaret Pleasant Douroux, 1941-

1. What shall I ren-der__ un-to God for all His mer-cies?____
2. All I can ren-der__ is my bod-y and my soul._____ That's

What shall I ren-der, What__ shall I give?
all I can ren-der, That's all__ I can give.

God has ev-'ry-thing; ev-'ry-thing be-longs to Him.

What shall I ren-der, what__ shall I give?

191 Trees

Margaret Pleasant Douroux, 1941-

M. P. D.

1. Trees don't want to be moun - tains, they just praise the Lord;
2. Winds don't want to be dark clouds, they just praise the Lord;

Moun - tains nev - er are val - leys, they just praise the Lord; The
Dark clouds nev - er are sun - ny, they just praise the Lord; A

Sun, the Moon and Stars are hap - py in their heav - en - ly space; the
grain of sand is hap - py sit - ting on a cool sea - shore; or

riv - ers and the o - ceans just keep mov - ing from place to place. So
e - ven in the hot - test plac - es mak - ing a des - ert's floor. So

192 We've Come This Far By Faith

Albert A. Goodson
Arr. by Thurston G. Frazier

A. A. G.

Refrain

We've come this far by faith Lean-ing on the Lord;

Trust-ing in His Ho-ly Word,_____ He's nev-er

failed____ me yet. Oh,_____ can't turn a-

round, We've come this far by faith._____ *Fine*

Verse

Don't be dis-cour-aged_____ with trou-ble_____ in your
*Just the oth-er day I heard a man say he did-n't be-lieve in God's Word;

*Optional: Recitation

life_____ He'll__ bear__ your bur-dens_____ And
I can say God has made a way, He's

(sing both times)

move all mis-er-y and strife. That's why we've
nev - er failed me yet, Thank God, We've

193 Surely God Is Able

W. Herbert Brewster
Arr. by Virginia Davis

W. H. B.

Chorus

Sure - ly____ sure - ly____ sure - ly____ sure - ly____ He's

Sure - ly sure - ly sure - ly sure - ly

Fine

a - ble____ to car - ry____ you thro'.____

He's a - ble, to car - ry you thro'. Car - ry you thro'.

Verses

1. As pil - grims all____ We here so - journ.____
2. He walked in - to____ the fur - nace door.____
3. One night He shook____ the Ro - man jail.____

We of-ten know not_____ which way to turn
With Shad-rach, Me-shach,_____ A-bed-ne-go,_____
Pris-oners stood free _____ on heav-en's bail,_____

For there is one_____ who _____ knows the road_____
He took the heat_____ out_____ of the flame_____
Yes, that same God_____ still_____ rules the world_____

Who'll help us car-ry, who'll help us car-ry Our heav-y load._____
I know to-day, I know to-day, He's jus' the same._____
His flag of truth, His flag of truth, Is still un-furled._____

1st Refrain
Solo

Don't you know God is a-ble,_____ He's a-ble,_____ He's

Response

He's a-ble, He's a-ble,

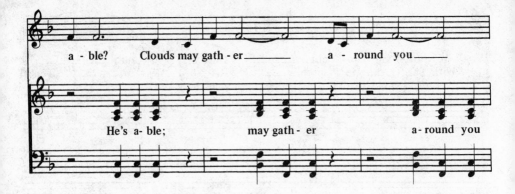

a - ble? Clouds may gath - er_____ a - round you_____

He's a - ble;   may gath - er   a - round you

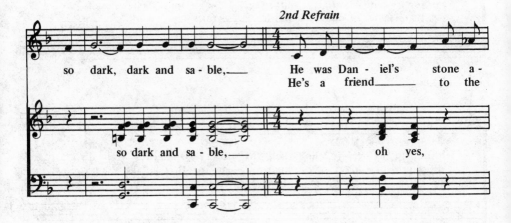

2nd Refrain

so dark, dark and sa - ble,_____ He was Dan - iel's stone a -
                                        He's a friend_____ to the

so dark and sa - ble,_____   oh yes,

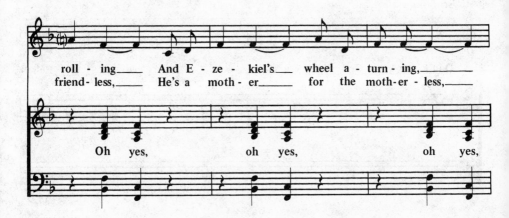

roll - ing_____ And E - ze - kiel's_____ wheel a - turn - ing,_____
friend - less,_____ He's a moth - er_____ for the moth - er - less,_____

Oh yes,   oh yes,   oh yes,

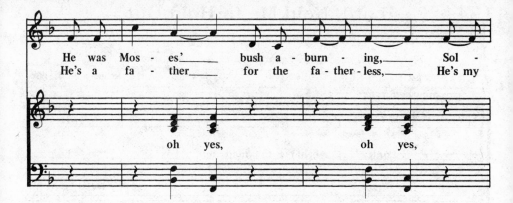

He was Mos - es'___ bush a - burn - ing,___ Sol -
He's a fa - ther___ for the fa - ther - less,___ He's my

oh yes, oh yes,

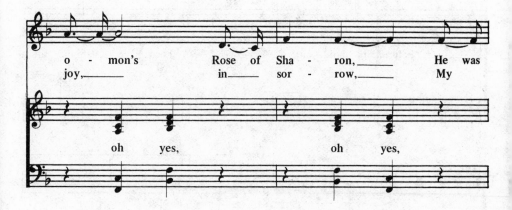

o - mon's Rose of Sha - ron,___ He was
joy,___ in___ sor - row,___ My

oh yes, oh yes,

D.C.

Je - re - mi - ah's___ might - y bat - tle ax.___
hope___ for to - mor - row.___

oh yes, oh yes,

194   Lord, Help Me to Hold Out

James Cleveland, 1932-
Arr. by Kenneth Morris, 1916-

J. C.

Lord,____ help me to hold out,____ Lord,____

____ help me to hold out,____ Lord,____ help me to

hold out____ un - til my change____ comes.____ comes.____

My way__ may not be eas - y____ You did not say that it would

be. But if it gets dark, I can't see my way,— You

told me to put my trust in Thee, that's why I'm ask-ing You. Lord,—

— help me to hold out,— Lord,— help me to

hold out,— Lord,— help me to hold out—

un - til my change— comes.— Lord, help me to hold out!

8va - - - - - - - - - - - - -

To Lulu Butler Hurse

God's Amazing Grace

Roberta Martin, 1912-1969
Arr. by Kenneth Morris, 1916-

R. M.

1. I was young but I re - call, Sing-ing songs was moth-er's joy   As the
2. Moth-er was so good and kind, Oft she told me   I would find   Not an -
3. At the clos-ing of life's day, Christ will   be   my hope and stay   I shall

shad - ows   gath - ered   at the close of   day,_____ And I'd
oth - er   who would   share my griefs and   woes,_____ So I
meet my   bless - ed   moth - er face to   face,_____ And I'll

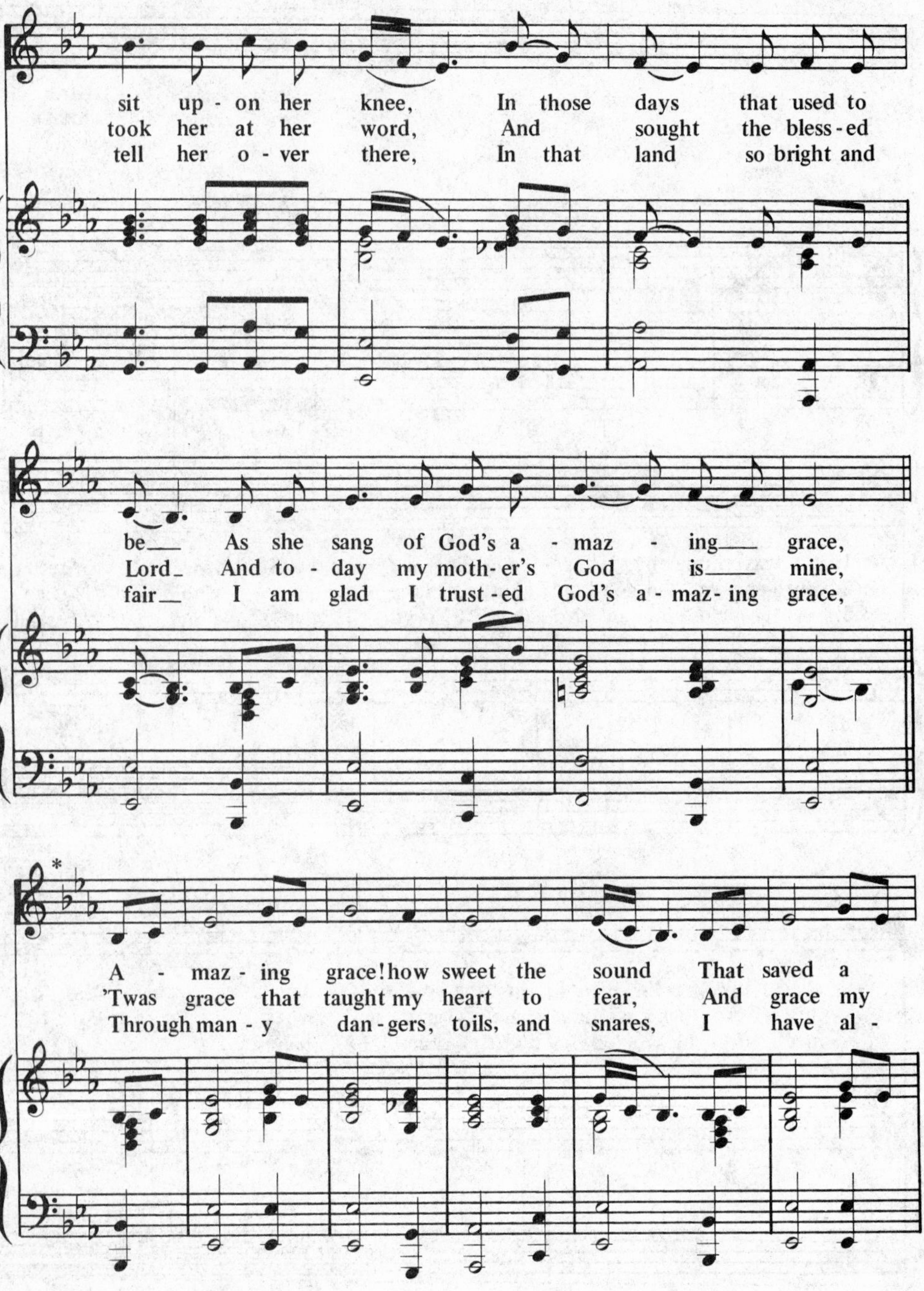

*Early American melody,
words by John Newton, 1725-1807.

wretch like___ me!___ I once___was lost, but
fears re - lieved;___ How pre - cious did that
read - y___ come;___ 'Twas grace___that brought me

now I'm found, Was blind, but now I see.___
grace ap - pear The hour I first be - lieved!___
safe thus far, And grace will lead me home.___

196 God Has Smiled on Me

I.J.

Isaiah Jones, Jr.

God has smiled on me, He has set me free.

God has smiled on me, He's been good to me.

Gm7   Bb maj7   Am7   G9   C7   F   *2nd time –*
D.C. al Fine

___ that I em-ploy,   He sends down from a - bove.
___ each day for me,   God is my all___ and all.___

2nd time –
D.C. al Fine

197   Only a Look

A.S.

Anna Shepherd
Arr. by Virginia Davis

Moderate, with feeling
Verses

1. On-ly a look at Je - sus, Oh, so bowed down with care,
2. On-ly a look at Je - sus, He proves a con - stant friend,
3. On-ly a look at Je - sus, Mer - ci - ful and true,

He has prom-ised to de-fend thee, He will all your bur-dens share.
He will bring you peace and com-fort, He'll go with you to the end.
Through the storms, through tri-als, He will lead you safe-ly through.

198   Soon and Very Soon

A.C.

Andraé Crouch, 1947-

1, 4. Soon and ver - y soon, we are going to see the King;
2. No more cry - ing there, we are going to see the King;
3. No more dy - ing there, we are going to see the King;

Soon and ver - y soon, we are going to see the King;
No more cry - ing there, we are going to see the King;
No more dy - ing there, we are going to see the King;

Soon and ver - y soon, we are going to see the King;
No more cry - ing there, we are going to see the King;
No more dy - ing there, we are going to see the King;
} Hal - le -

lu - jah! Hal-le-lu - jah! We're going to see the King.

King. Hal - le - lu - jah! Hal - le - lu - jah!

King. Hal - le - lu - jah! Hal - le lu - jah!

Should there be an - y riv - ers we must cross, Should there

be an - y moun -tains we must climb; _____

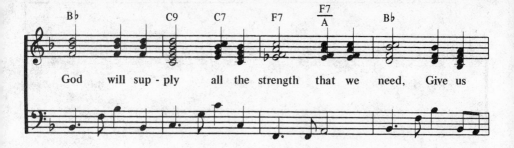

God will sup-ply all the strength that we need, Give us

grace 'til we reach the oth-er side. _____ We have

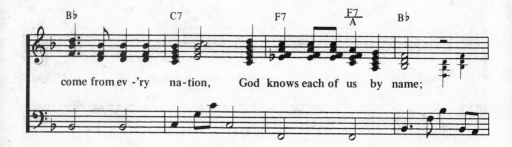

come from ev-'ry na-tion, God knows each of us by name;

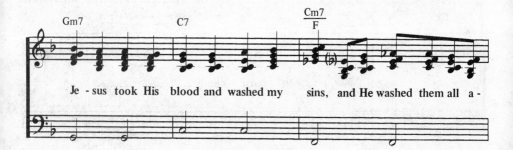

Je-sus took His blood and washed my sins, and He washed them all a-

way. Yes, there are some of us who have laid down our

lives, But we all shall live a - gain on the oth - er side.

lu - jah!

199

Lord, Touch Me

Martha Eason Banks
Arr. by James A. Jones
Special arr. by Clara Ward, 1924-1973

M. E. B.

Refrain
Smoothly

Lord, I want you to touch me,— Touch me with Thy ho-ly love.

Lord, come down and touch me.— Come down from

heav-en a - bove. Lord, reach out and touch me,—

Reach out and touch me with - in.— Lord, let good-ness touch me,

Fine

Thy touch will cleanse me from sin.

Verses

1. Some folks want trea - sures of sil - ver and gold, Some want to
2. Teach me to love___ and teach me to pray, Grant me a

reign___ with pow - ers un - told; But in my life,___ all
light___ to shine day by day; Just to a - bide___ where

D.C. for Refrain

that I can say, Lord, be my guide___ and have thine own way.
joys nev - er cease Will be great joy,___ such com - fort and ease.

200 Footprints of Jesus

L. E. C.

Lucie E. Campbell.

Refrain

Foot-prints of Je-sus, lead-ing the way, Foot-prints of Je-sus, by night and by day; Sure if I fol-low, life will be sweet! Saved by the prints of His wound-ed feet.

Fine

With religious fervor

1. They led to Beth-a-ny, there's where He stayed;
2. Once I was lost and He heard my cry;
3. Dan-i-el saw in Him a great roll-ing stone;
4. That's how I know Him, that's why I say,

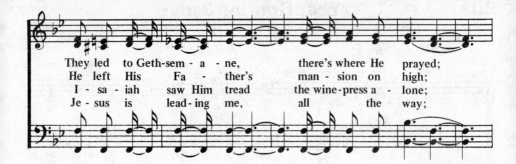

They led to Geth-sem - a - ne, there's where He prayed;
He left His Fa - ther's man - sion on high;
I - sa - iah saw Him tread the wine-press a - lone;
Je - sus is lead-ing me, all the way;

They led to Cal - va - ry, sal - va - tion com - plete,
He took my bur - den, and now I can sing,
If we some day our dear Sav - ior would meet,
I shall reach Heav - en's por - tals so sweet,

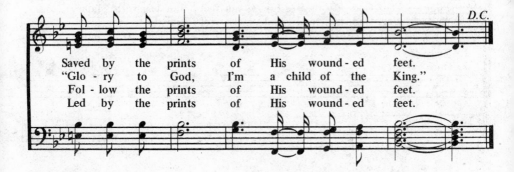

D.C.

Saved by the prints of His wound - ed feet.
"Glo - ry to God, I'm a child of the King."
Fol - low the prints of His wound - ed feet.
Led by the prints of His wound - ed feet.

201

Yes, God Is Real

K. M.

Kenneth Morris, 1916-

Slow with emphasis

1. There are some things I may not know, There are some
2. Some folk may doubt, some folk may scorn, All can de-
3. I can-not tell just how you felt When Je-sus

plac - es I can't go, But I am sure of this one
sert and leave me alone, But as for me I'll take God's
took your sins a - way, But since that day, yes, since that

thing That God is real for I can feel Him deep with - in.
part For God is real and I can feel Him in my heart.
hour God has been real for I can feel His ho - ly pow'r.

202
He Knows Just How Much We Can Bear

P. H.

Phyllis Hall

Slowly, with expression

1. We are our heav - en-ly Fa-ther's chil - dren And we all know that He
2. Think of the times you've asked the ques - tion Down in your heart now
3. Just praise His name al - tho' you're bur - dened, For there are bless - ings

loves us one and all; Yet there are times when we find we an - swer,
just what shall I do? Then you con-fide in your friends and loved ones,
He's be-stowed on you; In ev - 'ry way we must nev - er doubt Him,

An - oth-er's voice and call; If we are will - ing, He will teach us,
But they have trou-bles, too; There is a God who rules earth and heav'n,
These trials we must go thro'; Try to en-dure a lit - tle long - er,

sfz *pp*

His voice on - ly to o - bey no mat - ter where, and He knows,
In Him there's re - lief from ev - 'ry pain or care, for He knows,
And don't for - get that for each of us He cares and He knows,

203 God Be with You

T. A. D. and A. W. H.

Thomas A. Dorsey, 1899-
and Artelia W. Hutchins

Moderato

God be with you, God be with you, God be with you till we

meet a - gain, O___ God be with you, God be with you, God be

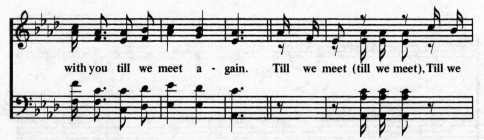

with you till we meet a - gain. Till we meet (till we meet), Till we

meet (till we meet) Till we meet our spir-its keep, Till we meet (till we meet)

Till we meet (till we meet), our souls in love do keep, Oh, till we meet

(till we meet), Till we meet (till we meet), keep us hum-ble at Thy `feet,

Fine Verses

God be with us till we meet a-gain.

1. If we nev-er-more shall meet you,
2. If your way is dark and drear-y,
3. Joy will un-fold like a flow-er,

If we nev-er-more shall greet you,
Cast your ev-'ry care on Je-sus,
If you trust Him ev-'ry hour,

God be with you till we meet a-gain,

Keep on work-ing for the Mas-ter, He'll be with you here and af-ter,
He's a com-fort when in sor-row, He's a joy for you to-mor-row,
Songs of joy will sur-round you, Ho-ly an-gels sing a-round you,

D.C. al Fine

God be with you till we meet a-gain.

Songs for Special Occasions

Praise God From Whom All Blessings Flow

Thomas Ken, 1637-1711

Lena McLin, 1928-

Moderately fast

Praise God from whom all_____ bless - ings flow;

(for rehearsal)

Praise Him, all crea - tures— here— be - low; Praise Fa -ther, Son, and

205   We Are Climbing Jacob's Ladder

Traditional

Traditional

from *The Dett Collection of Negro Spirituals,*
2nd Group

Arr. by R. Nathaniel Dett, 1882-1943

206 Blessed Quietness

Marie P. Ferguson

W. S. Marshall
Arr. by J. Jefferson Cleveland, 1937-
and Verolga Nix, 1933-

Joyfully

1. Joys are flow - ing like a riv - er,
2. Bring - ing life and health and glad - ness
3. Like the rain that falls from heav - en,
4. See, a fruit - ful field is grow - ing,
5. What a won - der - ful sal - va - tion,

Since the Com - fort - er has come;
All a - round this heav'n - ly Guest,
Like the sun - light from the sky,
Bless - ed fruit of righ - teous - ness;
When we al - ways see His face,

He a - bides with us for - ev - er,
Ban - ished un - be - lief and sad - ness,
So the Ho - ly Ghost is giv - en,
And the streams of life are flow - ing
What a per - fect hab - i - ta - tion,

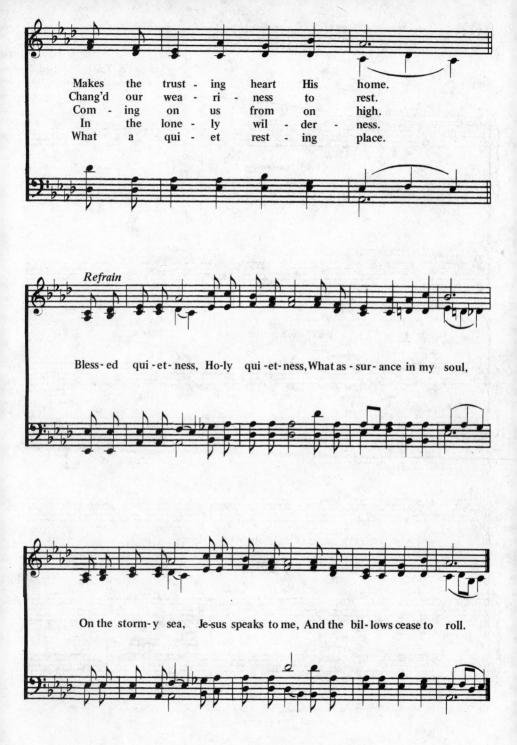

Makes the trust - ing heart His home.
Chang'd our wea - ri - ness to rest.
Com - ing on us from on high.
In the lone - ly wil - der - ness.
What a qui - et rest - ing place.

Refrain

Bless- ed qui -et- ness, Ho-ly qui -et- ness, What as - sur- ance in my soul,

On the storm-y sea, Je-sus speaks to me, And the bil- lows cease to roll.

207

In memory of my nephew, Rev. Gene L. Jones

Some Day

C. A. T.

Melody by
Charles A. Tindley, 1851-1933
Arr. and accomp. by J. Jefferson Cleveland, 1937-

Slow, with feeling

1. Beams of heav - en, as I go, Through this wil -
2. Of - ten times __ my sky is clear, Joy a - bounds __
3. Bur - dens now __ may crush me down, Dis - ap - point -

der - ness be - low, ___ Guide my feet ___ in peace - ful
__ with - out a tear; ___ Though a day ___ so bright be -
ments all a - round, ___ Trou - bles speak ___ in mourn - ful

ways, _____ Turn my mid - nights in - to days; _____
gun, _____ Clouds may hide ____ to - mor - row's sun. _____
sigh, _____ Sor - row through __ a tear - ful eye; _____

f When in the dark - ness I would grope,
There'll be a day _____ that's al - ways bright,
There is a world _____ where plea - sure reigns,
Refrain - I do not know _____ how long 'twill be,

Faith al - ways sees _____ a star of hope _____
A day that nev - er yields to night, _____
No mourn-ing soul _____ shall roam its plains, _____
Nor what the fu - ture holds for me, _____

And soon from all⎯⎯⎯⎯⎯⎯⎯⎯⎯⎯ life's grief and
And in its light⎯⎯⎯⎯⎯⎯⎯⎯⎯⎯ the streets of
And to that land⎯⎯⎯⎯⎯⎯⎯⎯⎯ of peace and
But this I know,⎯⎯⎯⎯⎯⎯⎯ if Je - sus

D.S. for Refrain

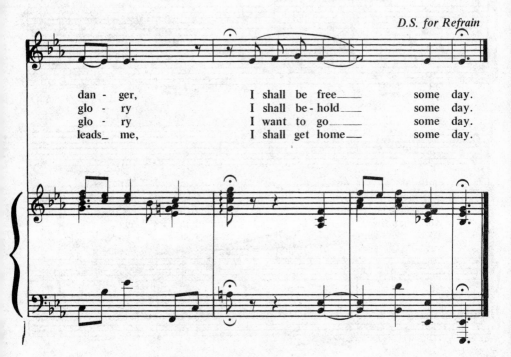

dan - ger,   I shall be free⎯⎯ some day.
glo - ry   I shall be - hold⎯⎯ some day.
glo - ry   I want to go⎯⎯ some day.
leads⎯ me,   I shall get home⎯⎯ some day.

Just as I Am

208

Charlotte Elliott, 1789 - 1871

WOODWORTH
William B. Bradbury, 1816 - 1868
Arr. by J. Jefferson Cleveland, 1937-

Moderately
Choir or Trio

O Lamb of God, just as I am, O Lamb of God, I come, I come.

Solo, Quartet, Choir or Congregation

1. Just as I am, with-out one plea, But that Thy
2. Just as I am, tho' tossed a - bout With man - y a

blood was shed for me, And that Thou bidst me come to
con-flict, man - y a doubt, Fight - ings and fears with - in, with-

Thee, O Lamb of God, I come, I come!
out, O Lamb of God, I come, I come!

209 They Shall Receive a Blessing

Ps. 24: 3-4-5

James Hendrix, 1920-

Who shall as-cend in-to the hill of the Lord or stand in God's ho-ly place?

Who shall as-cend in-to the hill of the Lord or stand in God's ho-ly place?

Fine

They that have clean— hands and have a pure— heart and have not lift-ed

up their souls to van-i-ty; and have not lift-ed up their souls to van-i-ty.

210 Lift Every Voice and Sing

J. Rosamond Johnson, 1873-1954
Arr. by Verolga Nix, 1933-

James Weldon Johnson, 1871-1938

1. Lift ev - 'ry voice and sing, 'Til earth and heav - en ring,
3. God of our wea - ry years, God of our si - lent tears,

Ring with the har - mo - nies of lib - er - ty,
Thou who hast brought us thus far on____ the way,

Let our re - joic - ing rise, High as the list - 'ning skies,
Thou who hast by Thy might, Led us in - to the light,

Let it re - sound, loud as the roll - ing sea.____
Keep us for - ev - er in the path, we pray.____

Felt in the days when hope unborn died;

had

Yet with a stead-y beat, Have not our wea -

fa - thers

ry feet come to the place for which our fa - thers sighed?

fa - thers sighed?

unison

We have come o-ver a way that with tears has been wa-tered, We

have come, tread-ing our path through the blood of the slaught-

ered.____ Out from the gloom - y past, 'Til now we stand at__ last

D.C. for Verse 3

Where the white gleam of our bright star____ is cast. *(piano)*

CODA *(After 3rd Verse)*

(piano) *(voices)* A - men.

In memory of my grandmother, Mrs. Matilda A. Perlotte

Amazing Grace

AMAZING GRACE
Early American Melody
Arr. and Accomp. by J. Jefferson Cleveland, 1937-

John Newton, 1725-1807

Very slow and free, with feeling

1. A - maz - ing grace,
grace that taught
man - y dan -

found, Was blind, but now I
pear The hour I first be -
far, And grace will lead me

see.
lieved!
home.

2. 'Twas
3. Through

4. When we've been there ten thousand years,
Bright shining as the sun,
We've no less days to sing God's praise
Than when we'd first begun.

Go Down Moses

Traditional

Traditional
Arr. by J. Jefferson Cleveland, 1937-

Freely

Choir

Solo When Is-rael was in E-gypt lan',

Let my peo - ple go;_____
peo - ple

Choir

Solo Op-pressed so hard she could not stan',

Let my peo - ple go._____
peo - ple

Go down, Mo - ses,

Go down, Mo - ses, Mo - ses, way down in E-gypt lan',_____

Go down, Mo - ses, Mo - ses,

Tell ol'_____ Phar - aoh,_____ Let my peo - ple
peo - ple

Solo *mf*

"Thus saith the Lord," bold Mo-ses said,

go.___ Ah!_____ Let my peo - ple go.___
peo - ple

mf

"If not, I'll smite yo' firs'- born dead,"

Ah!_____ Let my peo - ple go.___
peo - ple

mf Go down, Mo - ses,

Go down, Mo - ses, Mo - ses, Way down in E - gypt lan',___

Go down,

Tell ol'_____ Phar-aoh, Let my peo-ple go._____

peo-ple

Solo **ff** **fff**

Tell Phar-aoh, Tell Phar-aoh, Tell ol' Phar-aoh to

ff **fff**

Go_____down, Mo - ses, Tell ol' Phar-aoh to

Go down, Mo - ses, Tell ol' Phar-aoh,

1 **2** *rit.*

let my peo-ple go. go._____

rit.

let my peo - ple go. go._____

Dedicated to my music teacher, Mrs. Willie Lorraine Smith, Elberton, Georgia

Battle Hymn of the Republic

BATTLE HYMN OF THE REPUBLIC
American Camp Meeting Tune
Arr. by J. Jefferson Cleveland, 1937-

Julia Ward Howe, 1819-1910

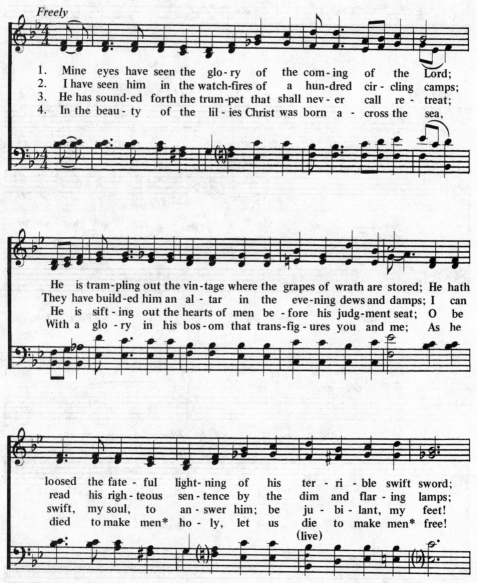

Freely

1. Mine eyes have seen the glo-ry of the com-ing of the Lord;
2. I have seen him in the watch-fires of a hun-dred cir-cling camps;
3. He has sound-ed forth the trum-pet that shall nev-er call re-treat;
4. In the beau-ty of the lil-ies Christ was born a-cross the sea,

He is tram-pling out the vin-tage where the grapes of wrath are stored; He hath
They have build-ed him an al-tar in the eve-ning dews and damps; I can
He is sift-ing out the hearts of men be-fore his judg-ment seat; O be
With a glo-ry in his bos-om that trans-fig-ures you and me; As he

loosed the fate-ful light-ning of his ter-ri-ble swift sword;
read his righ-teous sen-tence by the dim and flar-ing lamps;
swift, my soul, to an-swer him; be ju-bi-lant, my feet!
died to make men* ho-ly, let us die to make men* free!
(live)

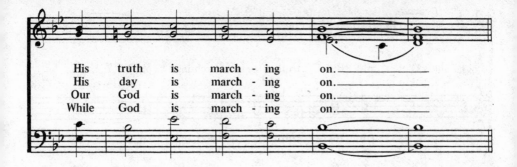

His   truth   is   march - ing   on.
His   day   is   march - ing   on.
Our   God   is   march - ing   on.
While   God   is   march - ing   on.

Refrain
Descant

Glo - ry!   glo-ry! Hal-le - lu - jah!   Glo - ry!

Glo - ry! glo-ry! Hal - le - lu - jah!   Glo - ry!

Glo-ry! Hal -le - lu - jah!   Glo - ry!   Hal - le -

glo - ry! Hal-le - lu - jah!   Glo - ry!   glo-ry! Hal - le -

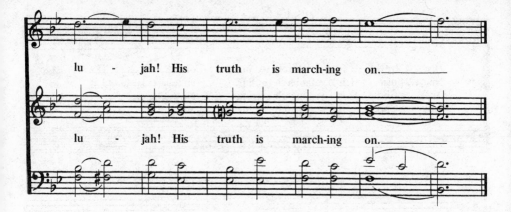

lu - jah! His truth is march-ing on._____

lu - jah! His truth is march-ing on._____

214   # In God We Trust

Unknown

Unknown
Arr. by C. Julian Parish, 1911-

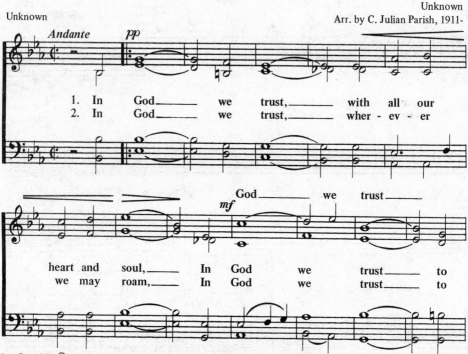

Andante   *pp*

1. In God_____ we trust,_____ with all our
2. In God_____ we trust,_____ wher - ev - er

God_____ we trust_____

mf

heart and soul,_____ In God we trust_____ to
we may roam,_____ In God we trust_____ to

215   My Faith Looks Up to Thee

OLIVET
Lowell Mason, 1792-1872
Arr. by J. Jefferson Cleveland, 1937-
and Verolga Nix, 1933-

Ray Palmer, 1808-1887

1. My   faith   looks   up   to   Thee,
2. May   Thy   rich   grace   im - part

*Piano accompaniment may be continued as in introduction.

Arr. copyright © 1979 by Abingdon.

Thou_ Lamb of Cal - va - ry,— Sav - ior di - vine!—
Strength_ to my faint - ing heart, My zeal in - spire;—

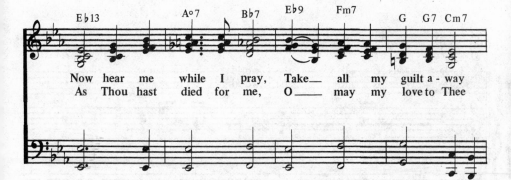

Now hear me while I pray, Take_ all my guilt a - way
As Thou hast died for me, O __ may my love to Thee

O __ let me from this day be whol - ly Thine!—
Pure,_ warm, and change - less be, A liv - ing fire!—

216 Jesus Is All the World to Me

ELIZABETH
Will L. Thompson, 1847-1909
Arr. by Verolga Nix, 1933-

W.L.T.

1. Je - sus is all the world to me. My life, my joy, my all. ___ He
2. Je - sus is all the world to me. I want no bet - ter friend. ___ I

Service Music
Introits
Let All Mortal Flesh Keep Silence   217

Liturgy of St. James
Trans. by Gerald Moultrie, 1829-1885

Morris C. Queen, 1921-

Let all mor-tal flesh keep si - lence, let all mor-tal flesh keep

Let   flesh   si - lence, let   flesh

si - lence, And with fear and trem-bling stand; Pon-der noth-ing earth-ly

si - lence,

mind - ed, For with bless - ing in His hand, Christ our

God to earth de - scend-eth, Our full hom- age to de - mand. A - men.

218 Let the Heav'n Light Shine on Me

Introit from *Five Choral Responses*
based on Afro-American Spirituals
by Roland M. Carter, 1942-

O Worship the Lord
219

Traditional

J. Jefferson Cleveland, 1937-

Stately and reverently

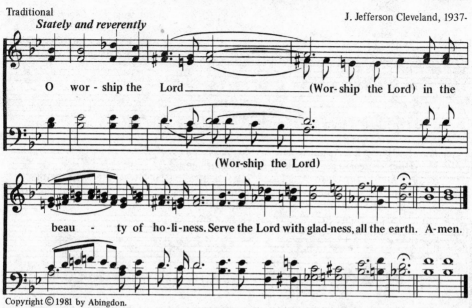

O wor-ship the Lord_____(Wor-ship the Lord) in the

(Wor-ship the Lord)

beau - ty of ho-li-ness. Serve the Lord with glad-ness, all the earth. A-men.

One God, One Faith, One Baptism
220

J. Jefferson Cleveland, 1937-
and Garel C. Smith, 1932-

Traditional

Slow, with feeling

p

One God,_____ One Faith,_____

and One_____ Bap - tism._____

221 The Lord's Prayer

Matt. 6: 9-13
Adapt. by J. J. C. and V. N.

West Indian Folk Tune
Arr. by J. Jefferson Cleveland, 1937-
and Verolga Nix, 1933-

Unison or parts

1. Our Fa - ther, which art in heav - en,
2. Done on earth as it is in heav - en,
3. And for - give all___ our debts,___ Hal-low-ed-a be Thy name.
4. Lead us not in - to temp-ta - tion,
5. Thine is the king-dom, pow - er, and glo - ry,
6. A - men, a - men, a - men,___

D.C.

Thy king-dom come, Thy will be done,
Give us this day our dai - ly bread,
As we for - give our debt - ors, Hal-low-ed - a be Thy name.
But de - liv - er us from e-vil,
For - ev - er, and ev - er,
A - men, a - men, a - men, a - men.

Chants

Hear Our Prayer 222

Morris C. Queen, 1921-

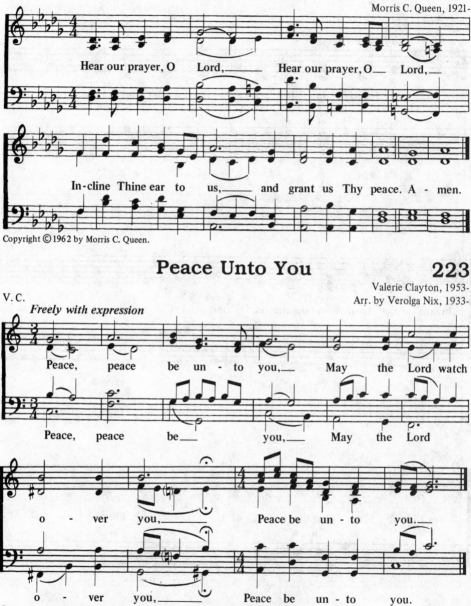

Hear our prayer, O Lord,___ Hear our prayer, O Lord,___

In-cline Thine ear to us,___ and grant us Thy peace. A - men.

Peace Unto You 223

Valerie Clayton, 1953-
Arr. by Verolga Nix, 1933-

V. C.

Freely with expression

Peace, peace be un - to you,___ May the Lord watch

Peace, peace be___ you,___ May the Lord

o - ver you,___ Peace be un - to you.

o - ver you,___ Peace be un - to you.

224 Let It Breathe on Me

Magnolia Lewis-Butts
Arr. by W. O. Hoyle

M.L.B.

Slow, with feeling

Let it breathe on me, — Let it breathe on me, Let the

breath of the Lord, now, breathe on me, Let it breathe on me, Let it

breathe on me, Let the breath of the Lord, now, breathe on me.

Verses

1. While I'm work - ing, Lord, in your vine - yard here, I____
2. When the path - way, Lord, I____ can - not see, When the

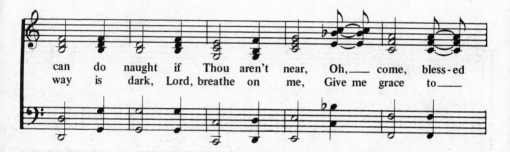

can do naught if Thou aren't near, Oh,____ come, bless - ed
way is dark, Lord, breathe on me, Give me grace to____

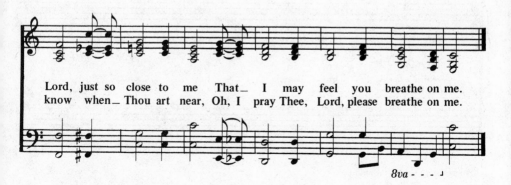

Lord, just so close to me That__ I may feel you breathe on me.
know when__ Thou art near, Oh, I pray Thee, Lord, please breathe on me.

8va - - - ⌐

225 O Lord, Have Mercy

Traditional

Traditional
Arr. by Verolga Nix, 1933-

1. O——— Lord, have - a mer - cy,———
2. Je - sus, I love————————— you,———
3. When— I'm in - a trou - ble,———
4. Hm hm hm hm hm,

O——— Lord, have - a mer - cy,———
Je - sus, I love you,———
When— I'm in - a trou - ble,———
hm hm hm hm hm,———

O——— Lord, have mer - cy,———
Je - sus, I love you,———
When— I'm in trou - ble,———
hm hm hm hm hm,

Have mer-cy, Lord,_ Have mer-cy, Lord,_____ on-a me._____
Have mer-cy, Lord,_ Have mer-cy, Lord,_____ on-a me._____
Have mer-cy, Lord,_ Have mer-cy, Lord,_____ on-a me._____
Have mer-cy, Lord,_ Have mer-cy, Lord,_____ on-a me._____

Spirit of the Living God

226

D. I.

Daniel Iverson, 1890-1977

Prayerfully

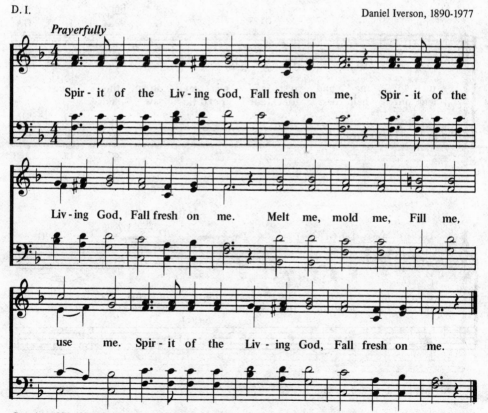

Spir - it of the Liv - ing God, Fall fresh on me, Spir - it of the

Liv - ing God, Fall fresh on me. Melt me, mold me, Fill me,

use me. Spir - it of the Liv - ing God, Fall fresh on me.

227 Shine on Me

Traditional
Harm. by J. Jefferson Cleveland, 1937-
and Verolga Nix, 1933-

Traditional

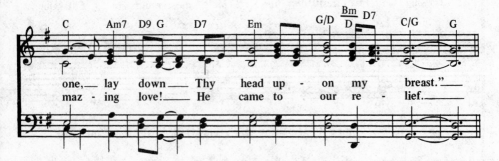

1. I heard the voice of Jesus say, "Come unto me and rest (and rest); lay down, thou weary one, lay down Thy head upon my breast."
2. With pitying eyes the Prince of Peace Beheld our helpless grief (our grief); He * saw, and O amazing love! He came to our relief.

* "God" may be substituted for "He."

Harm. copyright © 1981 by Abingdon.

Thank You, Lord

Traditional
Arr. by J. Jefferson Cleveland, 1937-
and Verolga Nix, 1933-

Traditional

Slow
Unison or parts

1. Thank you, Lord,_____ Thank you, Lord,_____ Thank you,
2. Been so good,_____ Been so good,_____ Been so
3. Love you, Lord,_____ Love you, Lord,_____ Love you,

Lord._____ I just want to thank you, Lord.
good,_____ I just want to thank you, Lord.
Lord,_____ I just want to thank you, Lord._____

Offertories

We Give Thee What We Have, Lord

O.H.

Odell Hobbs, 1938-

Moderato
mf

We give Thee what we have, Lord, Oh praise_____ Thy name.

230
Praise God From Whom All Blessings Flow

Thomas Ken, 1637-1711
Adapt. from Isaac Watts, 1675-1748
and William Kethe, d. 1593

Adapt. from John Hatton, d. 1793
by George Coles
Arr. by Roberta Martin, 1912-1969

Slowly, with feeling

Praise God from whom all bless - ings flow, Praise Him all

crea - tures here be - low. Praise Him a - bove ye

heav - en - ly host, Praise Fa - ther, Son and Ho - ly Ghost.

Peo - ple and realms of ev - 'ry tongue Dwell on His
Sing to the Lord with cheer - ful voice, Come ye be -

love with sweet-est song,
fore Him and re - joice,

To Him shall end - less prayer be
All peo-ple that on earth do

made,
dwell,

And end-less prais - es crown His head. A - men, A - men.
Serve Him with mirth, His prais-es tell.

Responses

God Is So Good
231

Anonymous

Anonymous

1. God	is	so	good,	God	is	so	good.
2. Je -	sus	is	real,	Je -	sus	is	real.
3. *He	saved	my	soul,	He	saved	my	soul.
4. I	praise	his	name,	I	praise	his	name.

God	is	so	good,	*He's	so	good	to	me!
Je -	sus	is	real,	He's	so	real	to	me!
He	saved	my	soul	And	he	made	me	whole!
I	praise	his	name,	He's	so	good	to	me!

*"God" or "God's" may be substituted for "He" or "He's".

232 Prayer Call and Response

MEAR
American Psalm Tune
Charles Wesley, 1707-1788, alt.
Harm. by William Farley Smith, 1941-

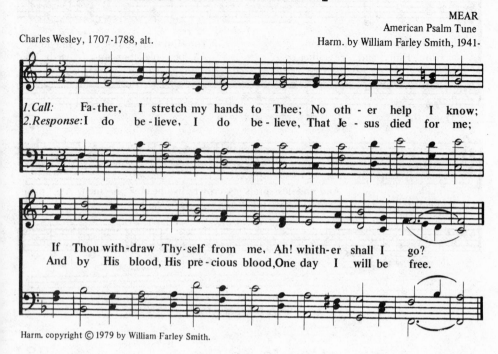

1. Call: Fa-ther, I stretch my hands to Thee; No oth-er help I know;
2. Response: I do be-lieve, I do be-lieve, That Je-sus died for me;

If Thou with-draw Thy-self from me, Ah! whith-er shall I go?
And by His blood, His pre-cious blood, One day I will be free.

Harm. copyright © 1979 by William Farley Smith.

233 He Is Lord

Unknown   Unknown

Reverently

He is Lord, He is Lord, He is ris-en from the dead and He is

Lord; Ev-'ry knee shall bow, ev-'ry tongue con-fess that Je-sus Christ is Lord.

Praise the Lord

234

Unknown
Arr. by J. Jefferson Cleveland, 1937-
and Verolga Nix, 1933-

Unknown
Freely

1. Yes,_____ Yes,_____ Yes,_____
2. Praise the Lord, Praise the Lord, Praise the Lord,_____
3. * He is good, He is good, He is good,_____

Yes,_____ Yes._____
Praise the Lord,_____ Praise the Lord._____
He is good,_____ He is good._____

*"God" may be substituted for "He." Other verses may be added at will.

Remember Me

235

Traditional
Harm. by J. Jefferson Cleveland, 1937-

Traditional
With feeling

Re - mem·ber me,_____ Re- mem - ber me, O Lord, re-mem-ber me._____

236 Come Here Jesus, If You Please

R.M.C.

Roland M. Carter, 1942-

1. No harm have I done you on my knees, (on my knees,) No harm have I
2. O Lord, have mer - cy on po' me, (on po' me,) O Lord, have

done you on my knees, (on my knees,) When you see me on my knees, dear
mer - cy on po' me, (on po' me,)

Lord, come here, Je - sus, if you please. ___ A -
A -
A -

men, A - men, ___ A - men. ___
men, ___ A - men, ___ A - men. ___
men,

Benediction

237

J. E. Rankin, 1828-1904

William Farley Smith, 1941-

Slow, with feeling

God— be with you, God— be with you, God be with you till we meet a-gain, by His coun-sels guide up-hold you, with His sheep se-cure-ly fold you, God be with you, God be with you, God be with you till we meet a-gain.

238 Doxology

Thomas Ken, 1637-1711

J. Edward Hoy, 1920-

With a festive air

Praise God from whom all bless-ings flow, Praise Him all crea-tures here be-low. Praise Him a-bove, ye heav'n-ly host. Praise Fa-ther, Son, and Ho-ly Ghost. Al-le-lu-ia! Al-le-lu-ia! Al-le-lu-ia! Al-le-lu-ia! A-men, a-men, a-men, a-men.

rit.

Used by permission of J. Edward Hoy.

The Lord Bless You and Keep You   239

Numbers 6:24-26

Peter C. Lutkin, 1858-1931

The Lord bless you and keep you; The Lord lift His coun-te-nance up-

on you, and give you peace, and give you peace; The Lord

and give you peace, and give you peace;

Lord make His face And be gra - cious un-to

make His face to shine up-on you, And be gra-cious,

you, be gra-cious,

and be gra-cious, The Lord be gra-cious, gra-cious un-to you. A - men.

Amens

240   Amen

J. Edward Hoy, 1920-

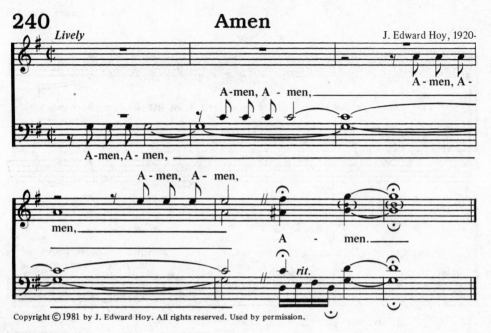

241   Amen

Verolga Nix, 1933-

Sevenfold Amen

Peter C. Lutkin, 1858-1931

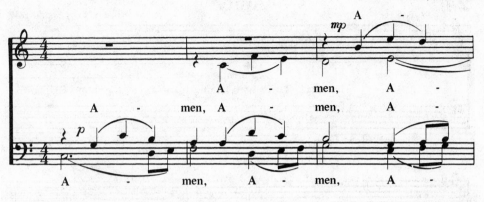

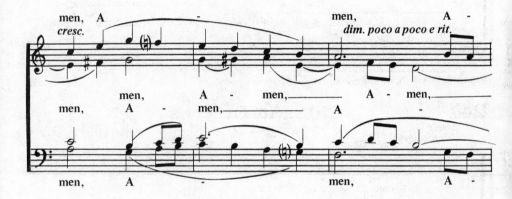

Communion Music for the Protestant Church

243   Introit

Issac Watts, 1674 - 1748

William Farley Smith, 1941-

S. This is the day   He calls

A. (That) the Lord hath made,   calls the hours. His own.

T.

B. Let Heav'n

Heav'n re-joice, let earth be glad, And praise sur-round the throne.

Copyright © 1975 by William F. Smith

244   Gloria in Excelsis

William Farley Smith, 1941-

Glo-ry be — to God on high, peace on earth to those of good will.

We praise Thee, we bless Thee, we wor-ship Thee, we glo-ri-fy Thee,

Copyright © 1975 by William Farley Smith.

Hymn—Hungry and Thirsty, Lord, We Come 245

W.F.S

William Farley Smith, 1941-

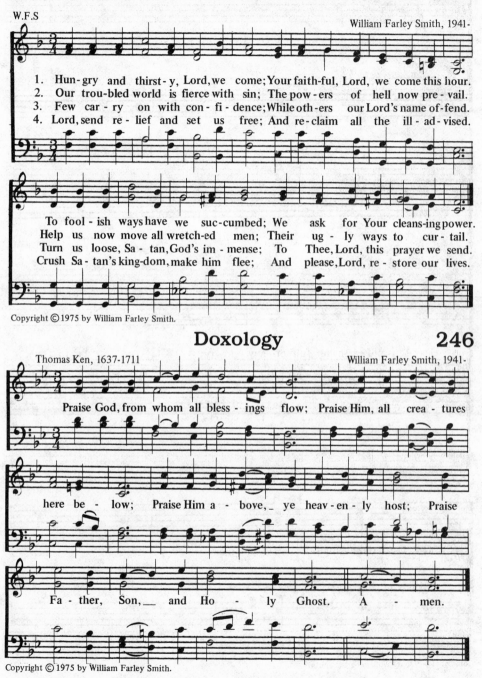

1. Hun-gry and thirst-y, Lord, we come; Your faith-ful, Lord, we come this hour.
2. Our trou-bled world is fierce with sin; The pow-ers of hell now pre-vail.
3. Few car-ry on with con-fi-dence; While oth-ers our Lord's name of-fend.
4. Lord, send re-lief and set us free; And re-claim all the ill-ad-vised.

To fool-ish ways have we suc-cumbed; We ask for Your cleans-ing power.
Help us now move all wretch-ed men; Their ug-ly ways to cur-tail.
Turn us loose, Sa-tan, God's im-mense; To Thee, Lord, this prayer we send.
Crush Sa-tan's king-dom, make him flee; And please, Lord, re-store our lives.

Doxology 246

Thomas Ken, 1637-1711

William Farley Smith, 1941-

Praise God, from whom all bless-ings flow; Praise Him, all crea-tures

here be-low; Praise Him a-bove, ye heav-en-ly host; Praise

Fa-ther, Son, and Ho-ly Ghost. A-men.

247 Sanctus

William Farley Smith, 1941-

Slow and detached

Ho - ly, Ho - ly, Ho - ly, Lord God of hosts;

Heav - en and earth are full of Thy glo - ry; Glo - ry be to Thee,

O Lord most high. A - men. A - men.

Agnus Dei

William Farley Smith, 1941-

Slow, well paced

O Lamb of God, who bears a - way our sin, we ask for mer - cy.

O Lamb of God, whose blood was shed for us, we ask for mer - cy.

O Lamb of God, our pres - ent help and friend, please give us peace!

249 The Lord's Prayer

William Farley Smith, 1941-

Very slow

Our Fa-ther who art— in— heav-en, hal-lowed be Thy— name,— O God,

Thy— king-dom come, Thy will be done on earth as— it is in— heav'n.—

Give us this day, Lord, this day,— our— dai - ly bread, O Lord,

And for-give us our tres-pass-es as we for-give those who tres - pass a-

gainst us. Lord, do not put us to the test, and keep our souls from_ e - vil,

For Thine is_ the king-dom, the pow- er, and the glo-ry, for- ev - er. A - men.

250 Benediction

William Farley Smith

Narrative:

The Lord bless you and keep you,

Narrative:

The Lord make His face to shine upon you and be gracious unto you,

Narrative:

The Lord lift up His countenance upon you and give you peace.

Index by Classification

Hymns

Negro Spirituals and Afro-American Liberation Songs

Gospel Songs

Songs for Special Occasions

Service Music

Amens

Benedictions

Introits

Chants

Offertories

Communion Music for the Protestant Church

Responses

Alphabetical Index
of First Lines (*Italics*) and Common Titles